Barbara —
Hope this speaks
to the sociologist
in you & maybe
also brings back
memories of those times."
love
Richard & Sharon
Christmas 98

# GONE TO AN AUNT'S

# GONE TO AN AUNT'S

## *Remembering Canada's Homes for Unwed Mothers*

Anne Petrie

**M&S**

**Canadian Cataloguing in Publication Data**

Petrie, Anne
    Gone to an aunt's : remembering Canada's homes for unwed mothers

ISBN 0-7710-6971-5

1. Maternity homes – Canada.    2. Unmarried mothers – Institutional care – Canada.    3. Unmarried mothers – Canada – Public opinion. I. Title.

HV700.5.P47    1998    362.83'9295'0971    C98-930079-X

We acknowledge the financial support of the Government of Canada through the Book Publishing Industry Development Program for our publishing activities. We further acknowledge the support of the Canada Council for the Arts and the Ontario Arts Council for our publishing program.

Typeset in Sabon by M&S, Toronto
Printed and bound in Canada

McClelland & Stewart
*The Canadian Publishers*
481 University Avenue
Toronto, Ontario
M5G 2E9

1 2 3 4 5    02 01 00 99 98

# CONTENTS

# *Introduction*

*"We used to pass the home on the way to school. We knew what
it was and had a morbid curiosity about the girls who were inside.
But we never saw anyone. Ever. I think they frightened us. The
whole place frightened us. Like we could end up there.
Thinking about it still gives me the shivers."*
– Barbara S., Vancouver

Up at the crack of dawn. Line up for your food. Do your chores.
Say your prayers. Don't talk about the past. No last names – ever.

Rules and regulations. Work and religion. Shame and secrecy.
What kind of a place was this? Who was it for? Where? When?

When was not so very long ago, only a few decades past,
times that many of us still remember well – the 1950s and
1960s. Where could have been an old house or maybe a brand-
new brick building or something make-do, such as a converted
army barracks. You might have found one – if you knew where
to look – in the middle of a busy downtown or secluded in a
residential area.

And who was there, lining up for meals and saying their
prayers? Girls. Just girls. Rich girls, poor girls. City girls, farm
girls. Girls as young as thirteen or fourteen; girls who were no

1

longer girls – young women in their twenties, sometimes older. But they were all the same in one respect. They were pregnant and not married. They were, in the vocabulary of the day, unwed mothers.

No one whispers about "unwed mothers" any more. Or about girls "in trouble" or young women being "knocked up." These are epithets from another generation. To be unmarried and pregnant carries no real stigma today. An adult woman can choose to have a child on her own and her decision is socially accepted, or at least tolerated. A teenager who finds herself pregnant may be considered to be part of a social problem, but not a pariah.

That's not the way it used to be. In the 1950s and early 1960s, we all knew what it meant to be pregnant and unwed. The warnings were loud and clear: your life would be ruined; you would be kicked out of school, perhaps out of home, and branded a slut or a tramp. You would bring indescribable shame on yourself and your family. You were supposed to just say no. But no was not a fail-safe contraceptive, and many girls found themselves pregnant – and mortified.

There were options, of a sort. Abortions could be had, but they were illegal, expensive, and usually dangerous. You could get married, but a shotgun wedding brought its own kind of shame – your family and friends either knew or suspected that you'd had to get married. If you could get married. Frequently the boy or young man ducked or denied his responsibility. Or the parents said no. Their daughter was too young to marry or this was not the son-in-law they had imagined. The idea of a girl keeping her baby on her own was almost unthinkable. Most often, and regardless of their class or economic circumstances, parents treated their daughter's pregnancy as a secret to keep. No one could know – not friends, relatives, neighbours, or schoolmates, sometimes not even sisters or brothers.

So the girls just disappeared. The cover stories were vague. "Gone to visit an aunt" was typical. Occasionally there was a family member in another city who could be trusted, who would take in a niece or a granddaughter, but often parents could not share the secret with anyone. The daughter was shipped off – from her own home to another home, a home to hide in until the baby came. A home for unwed mothers.

Every Canadian city and sizeable town had at least one home. Toronto had at least five, Montreal more than half a dozen, but few people had any idea that such places even existed. A friend of mine told me how fascinated and frightened she and her friends were of one home, which they passed on the way to school. Like children who are convinced that a house is haunted, they speculated endlessly on who lived there and why, and what it must be like inside. And, in a sense, the homes were haunted by the castaway girls hidden behind their walls and by the ghosts of the other girls who had passed through – and the babies they had given away.

What was it like inside those many homes for unwed mothers? Were they places of punishment? Rehabilitation? Did some girls find a refuge there, a sanctuary from a society all too eager to judge? What did they do all day? Whom did they see? How did they feel about their babies? Was it a time of shame and sorrow, or was there sometimes laughter from girls who had found a way to have a bit of fun? How did they plan for the future?

*Gone to an Aunt's* tries to answer those questions in the voices of the women who were there, women who include me.

—

The idea for a book about homes for unwed mothers came while I was watching the Robert Altman film *Kansas City*. It was set in the jazz age of that midwestern town – the 1920s and

1930s – and one of the many characters whose story wove in and out of the movie was a young, pigtailed black girl sent north by her family to have a baby. I wasn't paying particular attention to her until a brief scene – thirty seconds long at most – where she is brought to a home for pregnant girls, in this case pregnant black girls. Clutching her cardboard suitcase, she's taken upstairs into a room with half a dozen iron beds and as many hugely pregnant girls, who all gather round to greet the newest arrival.

When I saw this scene, I was mesmerized by something so familiar and yet so strange. I am not black and my own experience was a lot later, but I knew that place. I knew those girls and why they were there and what they were feeling. But until that moment in a darkened theatre, I had never seen a home portrayed before, not in a movie or a book or a play. I had not heard or even spoken of "those places" since I had been in one, thirty years ago.

In 1967, I went to the Salvation Army's Maywood Home for Girls in Vancouver – the same one my friend and her friends used to spy on. I was not as young as the girl in the film, and I came from a white, middle-class, fairly affluent family in Toronto. I had already lived away from home for my freshman year at Carleton University in Ottawa. But now I was pregnant, and even though social mores were beginning to undergo a change that would soon make the need to hide unnecessary and places such as this obsolete, the old rules held firm for me and my family. I was three thousand miles away, but my parents still feared discovery and social stigma. I, too, could not imagine being publicly pregnant. So I went to a home.

I found the experience excruciatingly lonely, and afterwards spent a good deal of energy trying to forget it. For a long time I thought I had. Because I was a couple of years older than most of the girls who were at Maywood with me, and because I had already lived on my own, I did not think I was like them. Even while I was there I thought of myself as more of an observer than a participant. I was studying Romantic poetry and eighteenth-century thought at the University of British Columbia. I didn't think of myself as just another "girl in trouble," asking the Salvation Army for help.

But the more I reflect on that time and that place, the more I realize that not only was I in trouble, just like the other girls at Maywood, but that I was profoundly affected by the months I spent at the home. When I think now of being pregnant in those times, and bearing a child that I would not keep, it is the memory of Maywood that brings it all back to me – the isolation, the sadness, the secrecy.

My story and the others in *Gone to an Aunt's* are from the time when I was growing up – the teenage years of the baby boom's first wave. Although maternity homes had been around since the mid-nineteenth century, they changed after the Second World War. Illegitimacy was a growing problem, and the number of homes increased dramatically – one of the unheralded postwar growth industries. The character of these places changed, too. Although they continued to be sponsored and run almost exclusively by religious organizations, they became linked to the emerging Canadian social-service network and affected by the new theories and policies of professional social work.

The need for homes and more homes – for a system of secrecy and hiding – could easily be seen in contemporary social attitudes. The same mentality that had sent women back home after enjoying a degree of independence during the war also sanctified the nuclear family and marriage. Sex outside that institution was a threat to the "Father Knows Best" world that was our model for behaviour. But ironically, other social changes almost ensured that an increasing number of unmarried girls would get pregnant. There was another new social phenomenon, that of the teenager. It was even a new word, and it meant a new if confusing code of behaviour, particularly sexual. The previous generation's ideal of adolescence – Mickey and Judy getting the gang together to put on a show – had been replaced by Annette and Frankie playing beach-blanket bingo, making up and making out. Such images from popular culture were often reinforced within the family. Ottawa psychoanalyst Marta Wassermann explains in her 1962 article, "How Mothers Mix Up Their Daughters for Love and Marriage," in *Chatelaine*: "On the one hand, mothers today are very often almost ludicrously anxious that their teen-aged daughters be popular – and basically, popularity, although we're reluctant to admit it, means sexual attractiveness. Yet these women idealize purity; they tell their offspring that they must be 'good' – that is, chaste."

Girls were under intense pressure to date and to have boyfriends. To be popular was everything, to "go steady," nirvana, and so the quandary arose: How could you attract a boy or man, or preferably a flock of them, and still follow the prohibition against having sex? It is not the whole story, of course, but no wonder many a boy pushed his luck and many a girl gave in. We were both getting double messages.

—

*Gone to an Aunt's* is not intended to be a definitive or even thorough history of homes for unwed mothers in Canada in the years 1950–1970, although I hope some graduate student in history or sociology looking for a thesis topic will take this subject on. I have found no academic studies about the homes in the decades after the war. The bits and pieces I have unearthed are all primary sources, and, like the homes, they were largely hidden, not necessarily intentionally, deep in the archives of churches and social-service agencies. I am sure there is much more to find.

But it is the girls' stories I am interested in telling. If this is a history, it is more a social, even a personal, one. This approach brings its own dangers. We all know that memory is not always accurate; the past is being seen through the lens of the present. So there may be inaccuracies in these pages. It's possible that the women I interviewed have misremembered details; I know I might have. There may even be distortions that have come from the loss and anger that so many still carry with them, even after thirty or forty years. But I have tried to search for balance, and brought to bear my journalistic standards. Nevertheless, it is our sense of what it was like then that I am after. How we all remember and feel about the time we passed in those secret places.

Finding women to talk about their experiences was not difficult. To begin, I didn't have to go any farther than my own high school for stories of girls who had "gone away." I tracked several of them down. I also simply asked around – women I met who were in their forties and fifties. Almost without exception I got something I could use. Sometimes it was just a memory of a home in their community, or the story of someone vaguely remembered. Occasionally a casual inquiry brought a very personal response, such as the chance conversation I had at the gym with a woman on the stationary bike beside mine. It turned out she had been at Rosalie Hall, the Catholic home in Scarborough. I also contacted adoption agencies looking for birth mothers from that time who might be willing to talk to me. Through the Internet I found many organizations and individuals involved in trying to reunite birth mothers and adoptees.

Not very far into my research I knew I had walked into a whole world of women's stories. Though there are the voices of many women in this book, I have concentrated on six, besides mine, all of us from different parts of the country, from different backgrounds, and pregnant at different times during those two decades after the war. Until I contacted them, few had thought much about the home they had stayed in, but they are eager to talk now.

Nevertheless, some of their names have been changed in this book – each woman has chosen her pseudonym. For reasons that I hope will become apparent, the pseudonym has both a first and last name. The names have been changed not so much because the women do not want to be identified. It is not the shame that they still feel, although that does continue. It is more that, even this many years later, they still fear others finding out – family who did not know at the time, current husbands and children, friends, employers. One woman, who is now a teacher, feels the moral pendulum may be swinging back and is afraid of how her colleagues and students might react. I have respected their privacy.

Until recently I had the same fears. Although my mother and father knew what had happened, my sister and brother weren't told. For thirty years the subject was never mentioned in our family out of a kind of mutual respect, a genuine desire not to hurt each other. We assumed it was over and best left alone. With my friends I was more open, not hiding the truth, but not particularly eager to tell them either. Almost as soon as I left the home in the summer of 1967, I found that the world had suddenly changed. In an odd way, no one cared that I had been unmarried and pregnant. In the 1970s and 1980s, birth control, a much more open sexuality, and the commonness of living together all made the old rules and strictures seem absurd. Now that we were "liberated," why would we worry about the old guilts and shames? No one considered that a past humiliation could cast a long, traumatic shadow. For a long time I felt the same way.

I never had any desire to make my story public and still don't. I am not very comfortable talking about myself. Part of what I like about journalism is that I get to ask the questions. There were times early in the research for this book when I felt I couldn't go through with it. I didn't want people watching me on television, asking each other, "Isn't she the one who . . . ?" I was afraid I might become some kind of novelty act or poster girl for unwed mothers. I was also concerned about hurting my family. I still am.

But I did continue. Partly it was out of professional instinct. I knew these were good stories that had not been told before. I felt that I was uncovering a fascinating bit of social history from not so long ago that had been almost completely forgotten – or never known. And I also came to believe that these stories are not merely interesting or curious, but important, too. To understand where we might be going, we need to know how it really used to be.

Our times are becoming more conservative. This is not entirely a bad thing. I could easily argue that there is some necessary correction to be made. We did not always handle the sudden sexual freedom very well. Perhaps we have not always been responsible about marriage and divorce. But simply to go back as we are now so often urged – to heed those who now trumpet the family values of the 1950s and 1960s – is false and cruel. Do we really want to return to those values, when they have so often hidden family secrets and shames, lives ruined and sometimes lost, loves abandoned or never known?

I do not like the victim culture of the 1990s and don't want to be a part of it. I don't believe claiming victimization accomplishes much except to pass on discomfort to others. I did not undertake this project to discover abuse, to lay blame, or to seek retribution. But I do hope I have something to contribute. I have collected these stories and told my own in the hope that it will remind us of how we used to treat each other – the harshness with which we judged and the harm of even the best intentions.

There is another reason why I wanted to write this book. When I was pregnant and unmarried and full of despair, my mother once tried to comfort me by saying, "Perhaps someday you will be able to help some other girl." I wondered then what she could mean. Help another girl "in trouble" or head someone off from the same "mistake" I had made? Either way, I did not get the opportunity. Until now. It is not some other girl, but grown women, I can now perhaps help in some small way. Not just the many women in this book, but also the many, many more – the thousands more – who still shrink from their own past, who have hidden away from others, and perhaps from themselves, a time and an event that is still burdened with guilt and shame. Women who are still "in trouble." I am not asking them to make their stories public, but I hope that, in hearing from others, they may feel less alone, less fearful, not so ashamed.

I hope this book will also resonate for the others involved at the time. Of course, there are the children, most of them adopted. I think they will want to know why they were given up. And then there are so many others – the mothers and fathers who were so shocked, the boys and men who so often fled. Maybe they will get some idea of what their daughters and girlfriends and lovers went through. Perhaps the connection will be more distant – a cousin or a neighbour or a girl you knew in school who suddenly went away. And if you think that you, your family, or your community was untouched, do not be too sure. There are many more of these secrets than you can imagine, usually kept long and well. At least so far.

As a final note, I want to explain my use of the word girls – a term that many feel is inappropriate or "politically incorrect," even dismissive and diminishing. I use it deliberately for several reasons. Many of us were truly girls – not even old enough to be called young women. But even the oldest among us became girls in the homes. Not only were we always called girls, we were not allowed to be anything else but girls. Although we were all having babies, the most obvious marker of womanhood, because we were not pregnant in the sanctioned manner we could not enter that secret sisterhood. We were girls, and we would stay girls.

# I

# *Waiting and Telling*

*"Lulu is pregnant. Lulu is over. She is no more."*
– Sylvia Fraser, My *Father's House*

—◆—

Whatever the end, every unwed mother's story begins in the same way: waiting. It was an agonizing, obsessive time spent counting the days – the late days – in every conceivable combination. Having your hopes shattered every time a trip to the bathroom didn't show the dark-red stain that, for once, you would welcome. You prayed desperately that it was not true, making deals with God to stave off the disaster that would ruin your life: "Please, oh please, don't let me be pregnant. If You let me off this time, I promise I'll never . . ."

But God wasn't listening, or didn't care, or didn't exist. Eventually, you had to face facts. The test – if you dared take it – would come back positive or, more likely, so many weeks had gone by that you knew you were pregnant. There wasn't any question any more, except whom – and how – you would tell.

We were girls brought up with a 1940s and 1950s version of the perfect marriage. A wedding in white would lead some months or years later to that breathless announcement: "Darling, I'm pregnant." This would be one of the great moments, perhaps the most joyful moment, of our lives. But for a teenage girl or a young, unmarried woman, the moment loomed as the most horrifying. You might have no idea how your boyfriend or lover would react, but you knew, or thought you knew, all too well how your parents would. It would be easier to say you had murdered someone; at least you might have the defence of your age. But not for this – this was the great crime of youth, especially for a girl. It meant that you had had sex "out of wed-lock." And now everyone would know. You were a slut. Pure and simple. There was no other explanation. Your parents would kill you, or at least disown you. Throw you out of the house – like that old cartoon of the stern father turning his daughter and her baby out into the blizzard. You could see your mother weep-ing, your father in a rage. It would be awful. You had done the unforgivable. It went without saying that it was entirely your fault. You knew the inevitable punch line: "What will people think?" You had been bad, as bad as you could be.

Those were the images in my head – I was sure I knew exactly what would happen, and so I put off telling anyone for as long as I could. For a while I couldn't even tell myself.

My story begins in the fall of 1966, in a fog – both literal and metaphorical. I had moved to Vancouver that summer to go to the University of British Columbia. Then the blue skies of a perfect July and August turned into a classic Vancouver special, one of those autumns of endless rain. My thoughts grew as dark and foggy as the weather.

I can still see myself walking across the UBC campus on one of those grey afternoons. A slim little redhead hurrying along – a young woman who looked as if she knew exactly who she was and where she was going. Not so much pretty as interesting-looking. My hair was cut short around my face, pixie style, and I had made my green eyes huge with great swoops of dramatic, black Mary Quant eyeliner and not one but two pairs of false

eyelashes. The whole effect was finished off by a short skirt, pat-
terned stockings, and a bright-orange leather coat. That's how I
was on the outside. Inside, my mind was turning like a wheel in
a hamster cage. I couldn't stop going over the numbers. How
many weeks had it been? What were the dates again? Did I have
them wrong? I'll count one more time. But my calculations
always came out the same. Without divine intervention, I had to
be pregnant.

Somehow I couldn't keep that fact in my head. It kept slip-
ping away into the fog. Maybe it was because, at the beginning,
it wasn't my worst fear. I was full of fears, and this was just
another.

Vancouver was my rebellion, or at least my way of declaring
myself independent. Until then I had been a nice girl from
Etobicoke – high-school president, public-speaking champion,
an A-plus student. Now I was more than half a country away
from that middle-class Toronto suburb. My excuse had been
the quality of the English department at UBC – which was
outstanding – but I had come here for much more than a good
degree. Filled with ideas of autonomy and self-discovery, I was
going to find out what I might become, far away from everything that had shaped me so far.

I didn't have long to wait. Almost the day I arrived I fell in
love. Truly, madly, deeply in the way that a nineteen-year-old
can, when she stumbles on her first great emotional adventure.
But the grand passion, which I had believed was a true union of
soul mates with no secrets or lies, was going very, very wrong.
The man, who had said he would give up everything for me,
seemed to be giving up on me. There were no flowers or love
songs any more. The hours that we could not bear to spend
apart just a few weeks earlier were now filled with his vague
excuses of having something else to do. Our plan to find an

apartment together had become a subject I somehow knew was taboo. I didn't know what was happening, or why. And I was afraid to ask – or tell. For a few intense months we had been together on such a metaphysical plane – our vocabulary, only art and poetry and music – that I could not imagine how I could ever find the words to talk to him about this very material bit of reality growing inside me. So I didn't.

Love, as I understood it then – and how it was defined for women then – meant total submersion. And so I had submerged myself in an other – a taller, smarter, wiser, older other – an other who knew life and would show me how to live it. I had given myself over entirely and joyfully. Without question, without doubt. This strange but wonderful new man had my heart, my mind, my judgement – and a good deal of my money. By the time the glimmer of truth began to rise from the fog, I had hardly any left.

I think I was always hungry that fall. At school I'd spend what I had on pie or cinnamon buns, anything for a quick sugar rush. An hour later I'd be exhausted and ravenous. I used to cruise the aisles of the local IGA, lusting after Chef Boyardee and Sara Lee, fantasizing about the food I would pick off those shelves when I had money again. Still today, I love grocery shopping and the luxury of piling whatever I want into the cart. But I wonder now whether it was simply hunger that I felt. Maybe those were the cravings – the pickles and ice cream demanded of the devoted father-to-be – that happily married, pregnant women get to giggle about. An ordinary pleasure of pregnancy that was not for any of "us."

If I'd been able to, I would have had an abortion. Legal or not. Dangerous or not. When there are no real choices, there are only desperate measures. But I had no idea how or where to look. Perhaps if I'd had more friends in Vancouver and more information about the city, abortion would have been an option. But there had just been the two of us – and he wasn't around any more.

On my own, I tried old wives' remedies. I ran scalding baths I couldn't even put my toe in. One night I stood for an hour at the top of the stairs at my boarding house, trying to get up the nerve to hurl myself down them. I remembered that a girl I had worked with a couple of summers before had told me about some pills you could take. At a run-down drugstore on the grotty end of Granville Street, I found what I hoped she was talking about. Every few hours I took handfuls of them, but after two days I couldn't keep them down and spewed them across the floor. I curled up in a ball on my bed and stopped trying to think or plan.

There were two things I could hold on to. The first and most important was that I was away from home. Three thousand miles away from Etobicoke and my family. I was going to be twenty on Christmas Eve. To me, the change from teen to twenty was enormously significant. I would be an adult. I didn't know how, but whatever happened, I was going to handle it on my own. I didn't need to tell my mother and father. I wouldn't. And I didn't. But my best friend did.

Sonja was the other thing I had going for me. She had been my roommate in the girls' residence the year I was at Carleton University in Ottawa. Sonja was smashingly beautiful, with clear, white, Irish skin and masses of long, curly black hair. She was also smart and daring and brave. I idolized her. Together we had moved out of our restrictive dorm, with its curfews and no-visitors rule, to share an apartment. And everything else. Kindred spirits, we talked effortlessly and endlessly about books and ideas and life and, of course, men and sex. We believed we should follow any dream we had. Sonja had encouraged me to go to Vancouver, and she knew from my letters about my great preoccupying love affair. I hadn't been able to write yet about how badly it had all gone, but I knew that, face to face, I would tell her everything. If anyone could make it better now, it was Sonja, and she was coming to Vancouver to share the Christmas holidays with me.

I met her at the train station, and it all spilled out within five minutes. By Christmas I knew the worst. The man who had said he wanted to be only with me, who had told me he was separated from his wife and waiting for a divorce, had lied. As simple as that. His wife, and a child I hadn't known about, had suddenly appeared. They were together now. I was really on my own.

Sonja's response had never occurred to me. I blamed myself for everything that had gone wrong, but she was angry, livid that someone would abandon her friend like that. She demanded that I tell him. If I wouldn't, she would. Reluctantly, I insisted on seeing him. And when I told him, he just sat there. He sat there on a wooden kitchen chair and said nothing. In frustration, I got angry at last – even hysterical. I started to scream and slap his face and pound on his chest. Then I began to weep. It was the first time I'd cried about any of it, and the tears brought a kind of calm and decisiveness. Now I just wanted him gone. I would not beg for help. I told him to leave, to get out of my life. I could tell he was relieved. Still silent and expressionless, he got up and walked out. For him, it was all over.

Sonja wasn't relieved. She knew that for me the trouble was just starting. She left a few days later, still worried about what I would do. How would I manage? Would I be able to finish school? What about money? I had no answers yet, though I soon would.

The following weekend, early on Sunday morning, the land-lord knocked on my door. There was a long-distance phone call. It was my father. He said he and my mother had had a call from Sonja in the middle of the night. I was "in trouble," she'd said, and she was afraid for me. "Is it true?" he asked. "What are you going to do?" Of course they would help. My mother would be there soon.

Their reaction was not what I had feared, but in many ways it was worse. My parents weren't angry or accusatory then, or ever. That wasn't their way. Perhaps I should have known, but at twenty my analysis and insight were limited. We had never been yellers and screamers or kissers and huggers. We were a typical Upper Canadian WASP family, rather proud, emotionally reserved, and concerned about appearances – values that I had grown up with and had now betrayed. At least that is how I saw my sin. As I listened on the telephone, I knew from their shaking voices that my parents were concerned, but I could only feel the waves of shame wash over me, shame not only for getting pregnant, but for having no other excuse than passion.

I had been worried, anxious, maybe desperate before, but it had been my problem. Now it was a family affair, and my little rebellion was just that – little, pathetic, and now gone. I was back in my parents' world, and I knew what was important. From their point of view, my reputation and future were at stake. Whatever I had wanted for myself now seemed mean and selfish. These were people I loved, and I felt I could not have done anything to hurt or disappoint them more.

I ran back upstairs, heaving with my first attack of morning sickness.

That is how my story begins. There is not another exactly like it. No one description would fit all the girls who found themselves pregnant and single in those times. Still, contemporary sociologists and psychologists tried to define the kind of girl who ended up in a home for unwed mothers. At a 1964 conference in Toronto, titled Out of Wedlock, the experts said we were "emotionally immature or neurotic" and "chronically adolescent," that we "often lacked a father" or were suffering from "unresolved Electra complexes" (Oedipus loved his mother too much; Electra was too attached to Dad). We were "probably middle class, physically attractive and well nourished." We were usually in high school, they said. Grade 11 was deemed to be our most vulnerable year. We "didn't have close relationships with girlfriends." And, although we may have attended church, we did not have "significant religious convictions."

I am not trained as a sociologist and have done no controlled studies, but from the dozens of interviews that I have conducted for this book, I've learned that the girls who ended up in the homes were as varied as girls are. They came from families rich and poor, from urban and from rural settings. Some were indeed in Grade 11; others like me had gone on to university. Many were already working, some as professionals – as nurses and teachers. Some had loving parents; others came from nightmarish families. Yes, there were missing fathers – and the trauma of a separated family in those days shouldn't be underrated – but did any postwar family see much of Dad? And there were certainly mothers who were not there for their daughters. If we were neurotic or emotionally immature, isn't that the definition of a teenager? As for sexual experience, some of the women I've talked to had had sex just once, others had taken chances before. Some were brutally attacked, some firmly seduced. I hope some were genuinely loved. There is only one generalization I can make about all these girls. They were the ones that got caught. That's our distinguishing trait. We got caught.

It is the only conclusion I can come to. Otherwise, I would have to believe that we were the only girls who had sex. But any honest look at those times tells us that the standard of no premarital sex was more a matter of rules than reality. Alfred Kinsey had already told us by 1953 that fully half of white, middle-class women (the only group he studied) had had premarital sex. We girls were fed a diet of Gidget and Tammy, and many of us – including me – longed for that kind of sugary romance. But we also knew about James Dean and Elvis. There was a dark and dangerous side to the times that thrilled some and affected everyone. At the same time as girls were supposed to be sweet and innocent, there was an insistence that they look sexy and be available. There was a lot more sex than people who yearn for a return to 1950s morality want to believe. No one who was there can forget the enormous pressure from boyfriends to "go all the way." We have no idea how many girls did. We don't know how many girls had abortions. How many had a shotgun wedding? Maybe some girls had the knowledge and the nerve to use contraception. A lot more were probably lucky. The girls who ended up in homes were just the visible tip of a very big iceberg. Of course, we wouldn't be visible for long. The moralists of the day would soon see that we were hidden away.

—

*Karin*

Karin Sorensen lives on the main floor of a large, renovated house in the trendy Beaches area in the east end of Toronto. Her living room is cosy with books and Oriental rugs, but her favourite place to talk is at the dining-room table. When I met her, that's where she was waiting for me, with a bottle of red wine and a package of du Maurier cigarettes, already half smoked.

In one way, Karin is not at all like the eighteen-year-old girl who found herself unmarried and pregnant in the fall of 1964. In those days she was always in motion – she enjoyed swimming and hiking and went all out for every sport. She loved to push herself physically and was always ready for any dare or new adventure. But a few years ago, in this very same apartment, she fell to the floor one night with a blinding pain in her head. It was an aneurism, followed by a stroke, and she was left partially paralysed. Her left arm is useless now, and her left leg stiff and straight. She can only get around slowly and awkwardly. Most of the time she is in a wheelchair.

Later that evening, as we started another bottle of wine and a second pack of cigarettes, Karin would tell me the story of how she got through the months in the St. Mike's "rehab unit for gimps," as she calls it, learning to talk and walk all over again. But first she told me about another place she'd had to find a way to cope with. Another place – thirty years ago – that she was put in for several months. In its own way, it was a sort of rehab unit, too – a place where she had to stay until she could make her way back into the world, until she was considered normal again.

Karin and I both grew up in Etobicoke. I didn't know her then, but I know exactly where she lived. In the mid-1950s, with the population booming, blocks and blocks of new, cheap three- and four-storey walk-up apartments grew like weeds north of the Queensway, Etobicoke's major southern thoroughfare. Until then, Etobicoke had been a suburb of single-family houses, and so these apartments quickly came to symbolize those who didn't quite belong. If you came from "the apartments," it meant you were poor, most likely an immigrant, and your mother probably went out to work. The apartments were on the wrong side of the tracks.

Karin's family had emigrated, but not from poverty or oppression or despair. They had left behind a solid working-class life in Denmark and a political system that offered them a lifetime of social security. But northern Europe was an uncomfortable place in 1951. Her parents felt the ominous presence of the expansionist Soviet Union. And her father had always wanted to travel. He had dreamed of going to Africa but had settled for

Canada – a new but safe place where he could get ahead and also give his two daughters all the best chances.

None of them knew any English, there wasn't a lot of money, and they would be starting over again, but the Sorensens had never put a lot of emphasis on material wealth. Education, culture, and equality topped their list of values. Karin's mother would have gone out to work whether they needed the extra salary or not. The Sorensens didn't care much about status or what people thought. They brought their girls up to believe they were as good as anyone else.

That was easier said than always believed in Etobicoke, and Karin was often embarrassed about where she lived. When she got to high school she knew her family couldn't afford the prom dresses and sorority memberships that were so prized. But still she was determined to make her way. She didn't have the classic Nordic good looks to get by on – her younger sister, Ani, got the blue eyes and blonde hair – but Karin was warm and easygoing and, like her father, was always ready to try something new. She made friends quickly, even cracking the defences of some of the middle-class girls who ruled her high school.

Boys really liked her. Karin wasn't prissy like a lot of the others, with their back-combed hair and coordinated outfits. She had no time for make-up or curlers. She kept her brown hair cropped short and was happier in pants and sneakers than in the skirts and girdles that were *de rigueur* at high school. As a teenager she grew long and lean and was seemingly always tanned. She projected a kind of sensuality, not a sexual provoca-tiveness, but she was comfortable in her body and that made her easy to be with. You can still feel it today. Her hair is mostly grey and her face is drawn, but the big smile still crinkles her eyes when she finds something funny – which is often. I could see why both girls and boys felt relaxed with her.

She fell for Bill in 1964. Tall, muscular, and blond, he was the classic dreamboat of those days. Karin liked him, and also liked the way the other girls envied her. He was older, already out of high school, which made him even more intriguing. Plus, he lived away from home. Even better, he had two English roommates who had crossed the ocean with the first Beatles records. Their apartment, Karin says, "had to be the coolest place in Etobicoke." There were no parents there to say what you could or couldn't do. Karin was entranced and did it all.

She had a grand time until she suspected she might be pregnant. Then her carefree life suddenly ended. "I was worried sick," she says. "I couldn't go to my family doctor so I just picked someone out of the phone book. His confirmation was devastating." How could she ever tell her parents this? She'd have to leave school. All her parents' dreams for her would collapse in ruins. They had made such sacrifices for her . . . and now? She had turned out to be just another bad girl from the apartments.

Karin decided to run away. She wrote a note to her mother: "I'm pregnant. Leave me alone. I'm sorry," and left it in a shoebox in her cupboard. "I put a few essentials in my purse and left the house like it was any ordinary day. But instead of going to school I went down to Union Station and took a train to Montreal. Montreal seemed a likely place to find work and then eventually to hide. I had this girlfriend whose older brother, John, had shocked his family just a few months before by moving to Montreal and living with a French girl. She was a folk singer, but we all called her his *chanteuse*. John and his French *chanteuse*. I thought she must be very racy and broad-minded, and I hoped that they would help me out in the interim." Karin paused, then reached for another cigarette.

"On the train I met a young Jew, not Hasidic, but very orthodox. I told him my situation. He knew the city well. He helped me find a place that first night and he fed me. His unconditional and unjudging kindness is something I'll remember always. A year later I received an invitation to his wedding. As for John and his *chanteuse*, they were very kind, but they couldn't really accommodate me." Staying in Montreal wasn't going to be as easy as she'd imagined.

Karin's plan to make it on her own wasn't going to work. So, after two days away, she phoned her mother and told her to go and read the note she'd left. Her mother came back to the phone, crying hysterically. She begged Karin to come home. Her father was calmer. He told her they loved her, no matter what; they would figure this out together. "Just please come back." She finally gave in. "I think that's basically what I wanted to do all along. I thought, They'll be so glad I'm home that they'll just forgive me for being pregnant, right?" Karin stopped for a second and then continued more slowly. "You know, I think that is exactly what it was about. That way I didn't have to face the music. In retrospect, it was an incredibly manipulative thing to do."

Perhaps her flight had been manipulative, or perhaps it was an understandable response to knowing the looks and whispers she'd have to face in Etobicoke. Either way, Karin stopped running. Her mother, father, and Bill all met her at Union Station the next day. They drove home in silence, no one knowing how or where to start. It wasn't until coffee was on the table that her mother, now more in control of her emotions, said the first words: "I hope you're not planning to get married." Karin felt immediate relief. Although she liked Bill, she didn't want to be married at her age. That would mean an end to any future she had planned. Fortunately, he felt the same way.

Her parents had another plan. Because they knew how Canadian society would judge their daughter, they wanted her to go back to Denmark. She could be with family there and, more important, in a society that didn't cast stones at unmarried, pregnant girls. There she might be considered unlucky or unfortunate but not bad. In Denmark, she could choose to keep her child or give it to relatives to raise.

Karin didn't say no right away. But she hadn't been in Denmark since she was a little girl. It was just a foreign country to her now. She didn't speak the language any more. It would mean being away from friends and familiar things and places. She had heard about homes for unmarried mothers – enough girls had "gone away" at her school – and a couple of days later she phoned the Children's Aid Society. There were such homes, she was told, in fact there were a lot of homes. There were also long waiting lists. "A lot of girls are in trouble these days," she was told. But they might be able to find a place for her at the Presbyterian home in Oakville if she could wait.

So Karin persuaded her parents to let her stay at home until there was an opening. They did not want to have to hide their daughter away. They hated the secrecy they would have to keep and the hypocrisy they would be a part of. But the Sorensens also knew these were the rules of the New World. As for Karin, now that the future seemed settled, she wanted her old life back for as long as she could. She swore her girlfriends to secrecy and made them promise the coming summer wouldn't be any different. She even persuaded them to go on a hitchhiking trip to Lake Simcoe, cadging rides and sleeping on beaches. Quietly, she hoped something would happen. Once, she dared everybody to roll down, fast, from the top of a very steep hill all the way to the highway. The other girls begged her not to, but she was determined. It didn't work. She still had to wait.

*Janet*
Janet Roberts gave me careful directions to find her in White Rock, the beach town about an hour south of Vancouver. Neither of us had a car, so I took the bus. I was to get off just

across from the Safeway on Ocean Drive. She would be waiting. It was a perfect summer day, and as the Fraser Valley rolled by I tried to imagine the woman I was going to meet for the first time in person. We had already talked on the phone for several hours, but I know from long experience in broadcasting that voices almost always deceive. Janet was sixty-one and had just taken early retirement and moved to British Columbia from Scarborough, Ontario. I didn't think she could possibly be as youthful as her light, girlish tones sounded on the phone, so I was ready to greet a plain, plump grandmotherly woman.

The only person waiting at the bus shelter had on a long T-shirt, purple tights, gold flats, and an ankle bracelet. Janet? "Of course I am," she said, as she gave me a big hug. I wasn't surprised to hear on the short walk to her condominium that she had just come back from a sailing course and the month before had been away on one of the Gulf Islands at a meditation retreat.

As we sat down on her terrace, iced tea in hand, Janet showed me the old photographs of herself that I'd asked her to dig out. It wasn't hard to see in the grown woman sitting beside me the bouncy little English girl walking hand in hand with her sister, both in school uniform. In the photograph, Janet's shoulder-length, wavy brown hair is held back by two perky bows. While her sister seems to be shying away from the camera, Janet is half a step ahead, eager, it seems, for what will happen next.

Next wasn't very pleasant. It was 1943 in Worthing, a seaside town in Sussex that was bustling with Canadian and American soldiers. Janet was eight years old, and seemed to have all the opportunities. The Robertses lived in a comfortable home. Janet went to a private school and took elocution lessons. The best times were after class when she would head for the beach. "Oh, I was crazy for the boys," she says. "I'd tease them and take their caps and make them chase me into the water. My mother was always mad at me because I got white salt lines on my shoes."

But life at home wasn't as good as it looked. Just a few months after the photograph of the two schoolgirls was taken, Janet found herself in a courtroom testifying about her parents' marriage. It's not something that she likes to talk about. Janet speaks quickly sometimes and she does so now, not wanting to give details. "It was physical cruelty – and I witnessed a lot of it" is all she says. She skims over the next few years when she, her mother, and her sister moved from one boarding house to another, with her father still a strict disciplinarian, even at a distance.

Janet's home life had been difficult, but at least she had her bearings. Now she lost them. "I didn't have much inner confidence in those days, but still I was a bit of a rebel." Insecurity turned outward, perhaps. There weren't strict school-leaving laws in the late 1940s, so as soon as she could, without telling her father, Janet took off. She was just fourteen. First she went to Oxfordshire to work as a mother's helper, and then up to London, where she trained to be a children's nurse. It was three years of hard work, but she loved babies. Ironically for what was to come, her first job was in the huge Bernardo Home, an orphanage that had sent hundreds of child emigrants to Canada in the first decades of the century.

Janet didn't like living in London – it was too big, too dirty, and too noisy for a country girl. And she wanted to "better herself," as she puts it. So she took off again, this time forging her father's name on a passport application. At twenty, now tall and pretty, she posed on July 4, 1956, for a last photo in England. She looks very much a young lady of the 1950s with her New Look swing coat, long gloves, and matching striped shoes and purse. She left England on the SS *United*. American president Harry Truman was on the same boat. He was sailing back to the White House; Janet Roberts was going to a new home in Scarborough, Ontario.

She had come to live with her favourite aunt. Because Vi was only fifteen years older than Janet, she seemed more like an older sister. As a little girl during the war, Janet had often stayed with Vi and her grandmother. Vi had a great time chasing after the overseas soldiers based near their town, and she would often let Janet tag along on dates to the park or the fair. Now Vi was in Canada as a war bride. She invited Janet to live with her, her husband, and their little girl.

Janet thought she'd finally found the secure home she hadn't had since she was a child. The little wartime bungalow wasn't big, but there was room enough for them all. Scarborough was a new community and Janet loved it right away. She could walk to the bluffs and be near the water, and there were enough empty fields to make it feel like the country. At the local church, Janet threw herself into work with the Brownies and the Guides. She got what was for her a perfect first job in Canada at Eaton's College Street store in downtown Toronto – selling clothes in the baby department.

Janet has many vivid memories from those first months in Canada. But one she can't recover is exactly how she met Rolf. Even though she was past her teens and was now twenty, she'd never had a boyfriend before. She was, she says, "really, really naïve about that sort of thing." Rolf swept her off her feet. "He was good-looking in that German way – curly blond hair and blue eyes. And he was rich. He owned his own store in Toronto that sold radios and TVs, and he drove a Mercedes. But he didn't spend much on me. I see that now. Still, I was pretty impressed. I brought him home to meet my aunt and uncle, and he became a real family friend. We used to all get in the car and drive out to the country to look at a lot of property that he owned. I thought he was a real catch."

It wasn't long before Janet was pregnant. Despite her nurse's training and all her work with children, Janet failed to read the signs. She didn't believe it until a doctor confirmed it. When Rolf found out, he told her what to do. Get rid of it. Have an abortion. Somewhere in the States. He'd find a name. Money wasn't a problem. Janet couldn't believe what she was hearing. She had worked so many years with children; she was, as she says, "crazy for babies." An abortion meant killing her own child. And she'd heard about Buffalo. It meant back streets and sleazy doctors. You could easily bleed to death. No, she couldn't do that.

Janet didn't once consider telling her parents. They had had such little contact over the last few years she wasn't sure they even knew she was in Canada. There was Aunt Vi, of course, but she wasn't much comfort. She was, Janet remembers, "just sort of embarrassed." Money was tight, Vi said apologetically, and she and her husband couldn't really afford to help, and well, really, they just couldn't have a pregnant girl in the house. Janet understood, didn't she? She would have to find some-place else to go.

Janet was used to being alone and having to figure things out for herself. But this was the worst. She needed help and there was no one to turn to. She tried hot baths and drank castor oil and orange juice, hoping that might do the trick. Her aunt knew what she was doing but didn't say anything. Anyway, it didn't work. Nothing worked. Janet started to worry that she may have harmed the baby. Futility fed guilt.

Janet had no idea where she would go or what she would do. One night she couldn't hold back the tears and she confessed everything to an older woman she worked with in the Brownie troop. Mrs. Evans was sympathetic. She didn't know much about it, but there was a place associated with the church, some kind of house that would take in girls like her. Janet grabbed for the lifeline. She wasn't an active churchgoer or very reli-gious, but this was her chance to hide as quickly as she could.

She went to the Bethel Pentecostal Home on Kennedy Road in Scarborough and asked if they had space for her. The elderly lady who interviewed her said she would try to fit her in.

## Loretta

Loretta Fournier isn't much bigger than me – maybe about five foot three – but she seems tall and carries herself with grace and elegance. At fifty-four, she's still slim as a girl, and I can't see a wrinkle on the expressive planes of her unlined face. Her calm dignity is matched by her voice – low, slow, and honied – the kind of soft tone that can lull a baby to sleep.

Loretta was almost a baby herself when she got pregnant at age fourteen. Today she lives in a modern bungalow in an Edmonton suburb, but in 1956 she had just come back from convent school to the small northern Alberta town of Peace River, where she had grown up. Most marriages in Peace River were mixed, and Loretta was part Métis. She was a gangly girl, all arms and legs and golden skin. From an early age she spent every moment she could with her father. He had been away fighting in the war when she was born in 1943, and when he came back he doted on her. He was the only good thing about home. After Loretta's baby brother died from congenital heart disease, her mother seemed to go out of control, drinking and disappearing for days at a time. When she was home, she couldn't stand the sight of Loretta, slapping her with any excuse. Her father tried to protect her, and the best thing he thought he could do was to get her away. When she was eight, she and her older sister, Victoria, were sent off to St. Joseph's Academy, a convent school in Grande Prairie run by the Sisters of the Holy Cross.

The nuns were hard on their charges. Girls who made even a little mistake were hit on the knuckles with a yardstick by the teaching Sister who patrolled the classroom. Loretta was singled out for extra punishment after the nuns realized she was Métis. She'd passed as white until her mother came to visit. Loretta could tell by the way the nuns looked at her mother's dark eyes and straight black hair they'd figured something out. After that, she couldn't do anything right. Loretta had always been shy and quiet, and now she tried to be invisible, hunching her shoulders and clutching her books tight to her chest. But despite the harsh treatment, she appreciated the security of the Catholic boarding school. "I believed in God, and I was happy in this place. I had my own bed, there was a bathroom. No one hit me. I could read." Books became her salvation. Loretta's father had told her she would get an education with the nuns, and Loretta knew that was important. Any punishment she got from the nuns was nothing compared to her mother's irrational violence. Loretta felt safe at St. Joseph's. She missed her father, but she didn't want to go home.

Sometimes she had to go. And it was on a visit back to Peace River for Easter 1956 that Loretta's life changed forever.

By this time, her father had left the house. Loretta knew it was probably for the best, and he wasn't far away. Her mother was a bit quieter now, but she had no control over her children. This weekend she was out at another never-ending party. Victoria, who'd left the convent school a couple of years earlier, was running wild. Loretta knew she was drinking and having sex. The little girl tried to keep out of her big sister's way.

One night that Easter she couldn't. Loretta was in her room just off the kitchen, sleeping, when Victoria came home from a dance with a crowd of noisy friends. Her sister tried to drag her out to join the party. Loretta huddled under the blankets. Then the door was pushed open again. "This big guy was standing there. Jack. I'd seen him around before. I said, 'Get out.' Then he said something about 'the darker the skin. . . .' I don't remember exactly what, but you know what I mean. He said, 'You're gonna like this.' He thought I'd be just like my sister. He stripped off the bedclothes. I kicked and screamed. He punched the hell out of me. Cracked a couple of my ribs and cut my mouth. He was really brutal. Afterwards, I got out through the window, with blood all over me, and ran down to my aunt's house. She went across the street to use the phone and called my dad's place. My dad and Uncle Bill came to get me and took me to the hospital. They stitched my mouth and wrapped my ribs. My dad said he was going to charge Jack."

Her father did try to get Jack charged, but it wouldn't stick. In those days the police weren't very interested in rape cases, especially in native communities. So Loretta was sent back to St. Joseph's, where she was watched. "Everybody waited to see if I got my period. I didn't know what any of it meant. I thought if someone kissed you, you got pregnant." When strangers arrived to take her away, she didn't know what was going on. They told her that she was pregnant and that she'd been charged under the Juvenile Delinquent Act with being promiscuous. She was now a ward of the court. From here on, the government would decide what happened to her.

She was taken away to Edmonton to a place run by the Sisters of Charity of the Good Shepherd – a locked facility, like a reform school, a place for both juvenile delinquents and kids who had been abused. Loretta says the nuns there were nice, but with a hundred kids and only seven Sisters, nobody could pay much attention to her. She just tried to survive. If that meant saying that she was a bad kid, too, she would. That's how you got along there. She learned that from the priest. He, too, was kind but nonetheless told her she was damned. "What I'd done only married people do, and I would have to hope and pray that God would let me into heaven." Loretta had been deeply religious, but now she couldn't find her God. He had abandoned her, she thought. She was alone and clearly worthless.

As I listened to her story, I remembered my own desperation that night at the top of the boarding-house stairs. But when Loretta stood looking down the two flights of stairs at the Good Shepherd, she wasn't trying to end a pregnancy – she still didn't really understand she was going to have a baby. Loretta was trying to destroy herself. The nuns found her unconscious on the floor below; she had broken her arm and several ribs.

When Loretta's pregnancy began to show, she was taken away in a police van with barred windows to yet another institution – the home for unwed mothers attached to the Misericordia Hospital. There were no padlocks on the doors here, but that's all that was different. Loretta was being put away again.

### Marie

Marie Benoit was putting the finishing touches on her daughter's wedding dress when I arrived at her home in Montreal. It was a delicious confection of tulle, lace, and hand-sewn pearls, which she had copied from a fashion magazine. I was amazed that she had sewn it all herself, but Marie said she had just picked up the skill as a little girl, watching her grandmother make everything from hats to lingerie.

Marie was born in 1943. Today she lives with her anglo husband in Pointe-Claire, but she grew up in the French community of Verdun in Montreal. She lived with her grandmother in a warm and loving home until she was eight, but when her grandmother died, she was sent off to live with a series of aunts, some of whom were kind and some not. Her parents had separated before Marie was born, and neither of them could have coped with a baby. They would occasionally try to get back together and insist that Marie live with them, but the drinking – her dad was a bootlegger – and their violence terrified her. Everybody in the neighbourhood knew what went on in the Benoit household. The part of Verdun where they lived was a tough few blocks called simply "the streets." But even there, the neighbourhood kids weren't allowed to play with "that Benoit girl." At the Catholic school she went to, Marie says, she was always the black sheep. "It was a terrible thing in those days, the 1950s, to have parents who were not living together. I remember one nun who told me that I was bound to turn out bad because my parents were separated."

Marie doesn't look like she turned out bad. At fifty-four, she's an attractive woman with a soft face framed with dark-auburn, shoulder-length hair. When she smiles there's a gap between her front teeth, which makes her seem quite girlish. She has a delightful giggle and an optimism and an enthusiasm that jar with the ugly details she tells me about her life. But she was always able to put up a good front. By the time she was sixteen, Marie says, "I had become quite popular. Because I could sew I always had nice clothes. I had a lot of friends and went to parties and dances all the time. All these things got me away from the turmoil I felt inside."

Marie left school as soon as she could, working at a variety of office jobs. At one point she joined the air force, thinking it would be a way to a career in nursing, but her parents were trying once again to be a family, and they persuaded her to come home. Of course, once again, it didn't work. Marie found herself back in a secretarial pool, this time working for an insurance company. It was 1961, she was eighteen and lonely. She fell in love with a young man in the same office whom she thought she could trust. They dated for two years, and were practically inseparable outside work. She even gave up her job when people started to talk about their office romance.

When Marie told François she was pregnant, the man she thought would never hurt her wouldn't believe it. He knew they weren't using contraception, but he accused her of having slept with someone else. Then he told her he was engaged to a girl in his home town. It was an arranged marriage, he said. He had come to Montreal hoping to get out of it, but both families were still committed.

I have heard this story from Marie several times. Each time, she tells it with a note of bewilderment. Despite what she experienced as a child, at twenty she still trusted anyone who promised to take care of her. But she was also used to rejection, so she didn't give François another chance to explain. She changed jobs again and moved to another apartment. She wouldn't take his calls or read his letters.

Marie's independence was short-lived. She was still pregnant and she found every escape route closed. When I recall my own difficulties with money, I can only think my fortune was great compared to Marie's. "I was starting to show so I had to quit work, and I couldn't get unemployment insurance because I was pregnant. Those were the rules then. When I was unable to pay my bills, the electricity was cut off and I knew I would soon get evicted. A neighbour would share a meal with me once in a while. In those days I stole food from grocery stores to eat. My little sister would secretly come to visit me and bring me food from my aunt's place. I really knew what hunger was in those days."

Marie fought hard to stay on her own because she knew exactly what the alternative was. Every French-Catholic girl in Montreal did. In 1964, only one thing happened to girls who got in trouble. They were sent to La Miséricorde, the place for the *filles-mères*, the girl mothers. That threat was held over every girl who appeared to be in danger of going bad – which, of course, meant every girl. Nobody used the word home for La Miséricorde. Everybody had heard the rumours of baby selling and slave work that were supposed to go on in the big stone building on St-Hubert. Marie would now find out from first-hand experience if they were true. The neighbour who sometimes gave her supper finally persuaded Marie to face facts, and lent her the bus fare to get downtown. It was time to do what all the girls in her state had to do. It was time to go to La Miséricorde.

*Linda*

Like Marie, Linda Chalmers was born and grew up in Montreal. She, too, was a Catholic, but because of the two solitudes that still characterized Montreal in the 1950s she had never even heard of La Miséricorde. Although her grandmother's family was originally from the Gaspé, she had "married English," and Linda never learned a word of French. But misery for young, unmarried pregnant girls came in both languages.

When I met Linda she had just celebrated her fiftieth birthday. She looks stunning. She wears her straight white-blonde hair parted in the middle, letting it fall to just below her ears. Her make-up is perfectly applied, and she has the Montreal panache with clothes. Having just turned fifty myself, I was frankly envious.

My envy evaporated as Linda told me her story. Like Marie, she came from a separated family, though it was a respectable, middle-class one. Her father had left when Linda was just a baby. Although her mother managed to keep up appearances, she did so only by living with an ad hoc family of various aunts and cousins. Linda was especially close to her glamorous Aunt Lila, a 1950s playgirl with a closet full of cocktail dresses. Lila always seemed to be going off with a new man, but she returned every time with something special for her favourite niece.

Linda got a lot of attention early on, as the only girl and the baby. Her mother liked to dress her up and show off her pretty daughter. But when Linda reached adolescence, her mother seemed to lose interest in her and Linda was on her own. "I was given an awful lot of freedom," she says. "Far too much, in retrospect. I was just allowed to go anywhere and do anything. When I think back now at the things my mother allowed me to do without any questions, it's no surprise that I got into 'trouble.'"

The "trouble" coincided with Aunt Lila's sudden death from a brain tumour. Linda was devastated, and perhaps it isn't surprising that soon afterwards she was smitten by the saxophone player in a bar on the Quebec–Ontario border. She had gone to the Cornwall, Ontario, area with her two older brothers. It was the early summer of 1961. Though she was just fourteen and didn't think she looked old enough to drink, nobody asked any questions. "They never asked for ID," she says. "They never did in Quebec. If you could breathe, you could walk into a bar. Quebec was wide open, especially if you looked nice."

And Linda did look nice, especially to the saxophonist. Teddy lived in Cornwall, not far from the border, and he played at the bar every weekend. Linda had had crushes before but never a boyfriend. Teddy was the first man to pursue her. At first he would come up to Montreal, then Linda started to visit him for the weekends and stay with a girl she knew whose family lived near where Teddy worked. They became a "steady" couple, and he persuaded her to do what, he said, other steady couples did. Soon, she was pregnant.

Linda remembers the scene in the dining room when they finally got up the courage to tell her mother. Her mother's boyfriend was there and he tried to say something kind, but he was shushed up. It seemed to Linda that her mother just sat there forever with her head in her hands. Finally, in slow motion, she pulled her fingers down her face, and looked at the two of them. She'd decided what had to be done. Teddy and Linda would get married.

Linda's mother didn't ask or seem to care what her daughter wanted. Mother knew best, and she was going to handle the situation. She confronted Teddy's parents and got them to agree to a wedding. A week later, mother and daughter were in Cornwall with an apartment rented and all the necessities for the newlyweds in place. All that was missing was the groom.

When they went to Teddy's home, he had gone. His stony-faced parents would only say he wasn't there any more. Linda has no idea what happened. "I guess he ran away, or the family decided he was not going to get married. He was about eighteen, you see. He might have been put up on rape charges because I was so young. He ran."

Linda's mother didn't stop to shed any tears. She took her daughter back to Montreal, leaving behind all the brand-new dishes and wedding linen. Then she went right to the phone and called the Catholic Services Agency. Linda's life was whirling far too fast for her now. It seemed like just a day later that she was on the move again, this time packed off to a wealthy family in Westmount. Her mother told her that she would live and work there, earning her room and board until the baby came. That was that.

In the 1950s and 1960s, unwed mothers were often placed by social-service agencies in private homes, called wage homes. There was always a demand for mother's helpers, and the cheaper they came, the better. There were lots of pregnant girls available. Many families felt they didn't need to bother with the race and language problems that immigrants brought when they could have a nice white girl to do their laundry and look after their kids. And, as a bonus, her shame meant this worker wouldn't get uppity.

"Light housekeeping and some babysitting" was how the job description usually ran. Maybe when the family felt they had something to give as well as take, these wage homes were good places to be. But even social workers at the time had their private concerns that the girls could be exploited. The wage homes were rarely inspected beforehand and follow-up was non-existent. I have heard many stories about families who took a girl in to cook and clean for her room and board and a bit of money, and they usually sound just like Linda's. "I had this tiny room. It was a wealthy couple, and they had a little boy. And the wife just used me like a maid. She was obsessed with shiny floors; I'll never forget that. They had one of those old buffers and I used to have to buff the kitchen floor morning and night. When she had people in, I would serve. She was really a bitch. Her husband was nice, but he was never there. And the kid was a little monster. I reached the point where I couldn't stay there any longer. I knew it was going to be nine months of hell. I called my mother in tears and said I couldn't stay there. So that's how I ended up in a home for unwed mothers."

### Beth

I could listen to Beth Holmes talk all day. Because I've mostly lived in Ontario and the West, I don't get the chance to meet many Newfoundlanders, and Beth is the genuine article. Her speech is peppered with the idioms of the Rock. Every woman is a "missus" and every man "that buddy there." Newfoundlanders have a different way with some words than other Canadians. For instance, "brazen." When you talk about a brazen woman there, it doesn't mean "shameless" or "flagrant" or a "Jezebel," as it does in the rest of the country. A brazen woman is brave, courageous; someone who doesn't take any guff and puts it all out there.

That's the way I see Beth, strong and self-possessed. That's how she looks, too. She's a handsome, middle-aged woman with short reddish hair and an open, tanned, slightly freckled face. But that's not always the way she sees herself. Though Beth says she's gained a lot of confidence in the past few years, she still often feels like the scrawny, hungry little girl who grew up dirt poor and mostly scared to death in Portugal Cove.

Portugal Cove is just nine miles from St. John's, but when Beth grew up there – she was born the same year I was, 1946 – it had the insularity of an outport. Beth has the acuity of a natural sociologist, plus a good dollop of the plain-speaking wit of her fellow Newfoundlanders. You can hear it as she describes the layout of her home town. "It was segregated into little spots. There was a place called 'up around the cove.' Only Catholic families were there. Then there was 'in the road.' That was for all the United Church people. Then down where I was, where the ferry goes to Bell Island, all the Anglican people lived that way. And we stayed with our own people, too. We didn't mix with other religions. We stayed with our own. Although, the baby's father was Catholic. I don't know how I managed that one."

When I asked Beth if her father had had a job, she just snorted. "Did he have a job? Sure, he had a job. Dad had a job drinking. He was an alcoholic. Still is. He was a fisherman, a carpenter, a boat builder, and so on. When there was a feast, there was a feast, and when there was famine, there was famine. Everybody knew that Dad drank and beat the kids, and beat his wife, and this and that and the other thing. It was no secret. I think that we had our own police force, for Jesus' sake. They were in there everyday. We all should have married cops."

There probably were enough Holmes girls to marry the local police force. It wasn't just Catholics who managed big families in Portugal Cove. The Anglican Holmeses had thirteen kids, and Beth was the oldest of seven daughters. Their father made the same assumption about all his girls. If they were with boys, they were up to no good. "Dad would always say to all of us girls, and not just me, 'Keep your drawers on.' That sorta still sends shivers up my spine. That was all you heard. 'Keep your drawers on' or 'Don't bring nothin' home here' or 'Don't come back here pregnant!' And you weren't even doing anything. So it didn't matter one way or the other because it was just a given that that was what you were doing."

"Keep your drawers on" is pretty limited sex education, so even at age eighteen, Beth didn't know enough to know what could or couldn't get you pregnant. She didn't think anyone would ever want her, anyway. I have a photograph of her as a teenager, with a long mop of hair falling across her face, suspicious of anybody who wanted to take her picture. Beth thought she was ugly. "About ninety-five pounds with dishwater-blonde hair," she says. She didn't believe it when her girlfriends told her she was attractive. As for boys, she didn't feel comfortable around them. But in the fall of 1966, she met one that she kind of liked. "I liked a lot of things about him back then. He was good-looking. He had a car. He had a few dollars to buy a snack and probably smokes. And he had a job. He worked in an office-supply company. That attracted me, too. Here's this buddy coming into the Cove in his car. A working man. A couple of years older. So we went around together for a while."

Beth didn't find out she was pregnant for five and half months. She didn't even suspect. She was working for a nurse as live-in help, and it was the nurse who saw the signs and hustled Beth off to a doctor. It was the nurse who told her mother. Beth couldn't really take it in. She was too embarrassed to tell her boyfriend. She says she didn't think they'd done the kind of "fooling around that got you a baby." Her mother (her mam, as Beth says it) was ready to stand by her, but neither of them could imagine telling her dad. They'd seen and heard enough to know what he might do.

It was the nurse who told them about Molly Breen's boarding house. She didn't know much except there was a woman in St. John's who had a big house on Wood Street, near the harbour, and who took in pregnant girls. She'd been doing it for half a dozen years or so. It didn't have anything to do with a church or the government. It was just a place and this lady who ran it on her own. Beth could go there, and Social Services would pay. Beth knew she didn't have any other choice. So she and her mam told her dad she'd got a new job up around the bay somewhere and would be living in again. Maybe he'd be too drunk to notice she didn't come home to visit. As for this Molly Breen person, Beth would just have to take her chances.

In Vancouver, I had waited, then told, and now it was time to make my plans. My mother arrived a few weeks after Christmas. We sat in her hotel room and smoked cigarettes together. I had never smoked in front of my mother before, but that day she just passed me the pack of Rothmans. Later, at dinner, she encouraged me to order a glass of red wine. She didn't ask about how or why I had become pregnant. Or by whom. I don't know if she didn't want to know, or if she was too shy to ask. Maybe, like offering me the cigarettes and the drink, it was a token of respect for my privacy and an acknowledgement of my ostensible maturity. I remember saying several times how glad I was that I was twenty. It had become my mantra. Look at me, I'm not a child any more. Of course, I didn't say that, but I hoped the message got through. I don't know. I was too ashamed to ask.

My mother had the name of a doctor in Vancouver, so we consulted him. He confirmed the pregnancy and we discussed options. Going back to Toronto was out of the question. There was school to finish, of course, but, more important, my brother and sister mustn't know, nor the neighbours or friends at church. Secrecy was essential.

I suppose I could have stayed alone. If I'd had a group of friends, what we now call a support network, that might have been an option. But that's hindsight. Even in 1967, pregnant, unmarried girls were expected to be invisible. I could not imagine myself parading around the university campus or anywhere else in Vancouver. What if I ran into "him" or his wife? When the doctor suggested a home for unwed mothers, run by the Salvation Army, I raised no objection.

The doctor was breezily confident. "Your daughter will do just fine there," he said. I'm sure my mother died a little: the Salvation Army? It meant charity. Religious fanatics. An organization for the down and out, not "nice" people like us. But I insisted. On the one hand, I didn't care what happened. On the other hand, I felt it would be the right place for a girl like me. I wasn't "nice" any more; I deserved to be hidden away. Or at least that's what I sensed everybody would think, even if they were too polite to say so. All of the disagreeable aspects of the Army seemed to me to make their home exactly the right place to go. The punishment would fit the crime. To ask for any special treatment would be selfish. I had tried my wings, soared for a moment, and then crash-landed. Now I only wanted to be a good daughter. In some convoluted way, I thought that putting myself in a home would show my parents how sorry I was for all the trouble I had caused them. It is sad that we could not talk all this out more openly, but that's the way we were. That's the way the world was, too, then.

—

Waiting and telling. Telling and hiding. That's how it went for all seven of us – me in Vancouver, Karin in Toronto, Janet in Scarborough, Loretta in northern Alberta, Marie and Linda in Montreal, Beth in St. John's. And we were just a few of the thousands of girls in the 1950s and 1960s who made the same kind of journey. There are countless other stories to tell. Many girls were abruptly thrown out of school. Lily M. was in Grade 12 in Calgary when, at three months, she started to show. The vice-principal called her into his office and told her how "disappointed" he was in her. "It was worse than my father, who yelled and screamed, because this was so much more formal," she says. Some girls were thrown out of the house. Allie F. in Vancouver told her parents one night, then came down the next morning for breakfast to find a note saying that she wouldn't be expected for dinner again, ever. Or Laura D., also from British Columbia, whose father's reaction was to get drunk and demand to know where her boyfriend lived. "He wanted to go and shoot him," Laura says. Others went much further along the abortion route than I or Janet did. Louella S. in Regina got all the way to the "doctor's" door in Chinatown, then turned and ran, with him frantically chasing her down the alley, afraid she was going to turn him in to the police.

For all of us there were long months to wait until a home would accept us. In Toronto, Arlene V. told me she wore two girdles for months in an attempt to look normal. One night at a dance her partner got a sharp jab from the kicking baby. He didn't figure it out, but somebody else did and spray-painted "Your daughter's pregnant" across the garage door at home.

That all of us were so easily and promptly hidden away – or felt we had to hide ourselves away – still hurts many of the women I talked to. "Why didn't my family let me stay at home? Why didn't they just say, 'To hell with the neighbours and everybody else'?" Good questions, and they all have their answer in the times. Somebody could spray-paint your garage door. As Joni Mitchell has told the press about her unwed pregnancy in 1965, "The main thing at the time was to conceal it. The scandal was so intense. A daughter could do nothing more disgraceful. It ruined you in a social sense. You have no idea what the stigma was."

Whatever liberal currents might have been stirring – and they were at least by the mid-1960s – society still officially condemned sex outside of marriage, and rejected any obvious evidence – like a swollen stomach – that this rule had been broken. The cliché was true: an unwed pregnancy meant a girl's life was over in many ways. She couldn't go back to school, she would be ruined for marriage. But with a convincing story, maybe friends and neighbours might really believe she had gone to an aunt's. Some parents just wanted to get rid of their daughter and her problem. For others, hiding offered at least the chance for her to resume a normal life later on. It is hard to imagine a mother or father brave enough to flout the massive prejudice of the day against unwed mothers. It is easy to see how sending your daughter away to a home – where at least there was food, shelter, and safety – could seem the best option. If it also meant shame and punishment that would scar her for many years, perhaps even forever, well, nobody said anything about that.

2

# A Home to Hide

> "A maternity home can offer much to the unmarried mother whose
> own home is not a good place for her during her pregnancy. There she
> may live in an atmosphere of acceptance and cheerfulness, in which
> she may develop interests and skills, and enjoy companionship.
> The calm orderliness of a routine designed for harmony may give
> her a chance, with the help of a caseworker, to think over her
> situation and understand some of the things that have
> contributed to her becoming an unmarried mother."
> – *Social Services for Unmarried Mothers*, Canadian
> Welfare Council, 1957

I had no idea where I was going when the social worker from
the Vancouver Children's Aid Society called for me one rainy
afternoon. By this time it was mid-March, my waistline was
thickening noticeably, and I was relieved to be getting away. I
had left all the arrangements to the social worker. I had not seen
the Salvation Army home I would be going to. I knew nothing
about it. Wanting only to get it all over with, I tried not to think
about what might be waiting for me. I only knew that I was
already afraid of being detected. I stood on the curb, a small

from the mid-1960s lists twenty in Ontario alone. For 1967, I have counted more than thirty others from British Columbia to Newfoundland. Plus it's likely there were many unofficial homes such as Molly Breen's boarding house in St. John's. There was the widow outside Moncton who rented rooms to pregnant girls to earn extra money. In Calgary, a wealthy Catholic couple who lived in an old Mount Royal mansion with their twelve kids always kept one or two rooms for a girl in trouble. In Edmonton, the Beulah Home was run privately by a group of Christian women. It's impossible to get an accurate number of the places there were for girls to hide. Even though some provinces provided some government funding – by the late 1960s, after the Charitable Institutions Act was amended, Ontario was paying up to eight dollars per girl per day – there was often no provincial and, as far as I discovered, no national registry of names or numbers. Even the religious institutions that ran most of these homes often kept no central records, leaving the establishment and operation of a shelter to the local district or parish.

The first homes in Canada were opened in the mid-nineteenth century in Quebec. Before then, an unmarried, pregnant girl or woman had to fend for herself. She is portrayed in literature as Nathaniel Hawthorne's Hester Prynne or Thomas Hardy's Tess, driven out of her community with nowhere to turn. Real life was not much different. Recourses were few for such women. Proving paternity – if she dared to try – all too often was a matter of her word against his. Her visible shame undermined her credibility, and she couldn't count on getting the marriage she might have been promised. Domestic service was sometimes an option, and in rare cases the girl would be sheltered by her family. Some girls would try to obtain, or more probably induce, abortions. Often the very desperate would contrive to conceal their pregnancies, and either abandon the child or smother it at birth.

Contemporary newspaper reports of passive and active infanticide roused the devout to action. In the Roman Catholic Church, Archbishop Ignace Bourget of Montreal took the first step. In 1840, he asked a widowed mother of eleven children, Rosalie Cadron Jetté, to take a single, pregnant woman into her home. More requests followed, and finally, when her children were on their own, he asked her to leave her family and to rent a house and manage it as a home for unwed mothers. In 1848, exalted by her mission, Madame Jetté and seven other women formed the congregation of Les Soeurs de la Miséricorde, an order devoted exclusively to the care of women who needed to hide. Their passion made the Sisters eager to open homes wherever they were called.

The first invitation to the Sisters from outside Montreal came from the Catholic Archbishop of Toronto in 1914. But the home they opened on Bond Street soon proved too small. As demand grew after the first World War, St. Mary's Infants Home moved from its single house on Bond to two large, side-by-side properties at Jarvis and Isabella streets. After the Second World War, the numbers of unwed mothers shot up. This time the order decided to build. In 1956, it opened a new facility in Scarborough. The large, modern home was named Rosalie Hall to honour the order's founder. By the end of the 1960s, the order had ten homes across Canada, six of them in Quebec.

Over the years, the Sisters had also opened hospitals adjacent to their homes, first for maternity care, then for general surgery. The Misericordia hospitals became well known in Ottawa, Winnipeg, and Edmonton, and in Milwaukee and New York. Much less well known were the homes attached to them to house the girls whose plight had started the Sisters' work in health and medicine.

Les Soeurs de la Miséricorde weren't the only Roman Catholics running homes. Other orders and parishes opened their own homes, quite independent from the Miséricorde "chain," in large cities such as Vancouver and small ones such as Chatham, Ontario.

The Protestants were quick to follow the Roman Catholics. Their first shelters were the private projects of evangelical and philanthropic women who seized upon "fallen women" as a group needing their attention. In Toronto, as an anonymous, early history of social welfare agencies in the city states, the Magdalen Asylum was established in 1853 to provide health care and moral reform to "fallen women who begged on the street, sold small trifles and became so besotted and helpless they would lie in the gutter." In 1867, the Haven and Prison Gate Mission opened to take in needy women of all kinds, including unmarried, pregnant girls. The mission's administrators patrolled streets, police courts, jails, and reformatories, urging women to go to the Haven on release until they were better prepared to enter society. A group of privileged mothers opened the Toronto Infants Home in 1875 as a sort of day nursery and orphanage to help wet nurses who had had to abandon their own children to feed the babies of the wealthy. The home was established to care for infants, but it soon developed into a refuge for unmarried, pregnant women.

By the start of the twentieth century, the organized churches had taken over the privately run homes. In 1901, a young Irish immigrant girl came to a men's hostel in Toronto seeking shelter. The prominent Massey family took her in. Her plight opened the family's eyes, and they later built a residence. Named after a son, Victor Massey, it primarily served young or pregnant immigrant girls from the British Isles. It was taken over by the United Church in the late 1920s. Soon afterwards, the United Church also opened homes in Winnipeg and Burnaby, British Columbia. By late 1950, they were operating six "redemptive homes for unmarried mothers" in Canada.

Other denominations joined the maternity home movement. Anglican involvement started at St. Thomas Church, Huron, during Lent in 1911. A committee report stated, "There is no such home in Canada operated by the Church of England, a great and serious reproach to us all." Humewood House, named for the small road on which it sat near the corner of St. Clair Avenue and Vaughan Road, opened in 1912, expanding in 1925 and again in 1952. The Anglicans also co-sponsored the United Church home in Winnipeg and ran a small residence, St. John's, in Edmonton. As the numbers of unwed mothers kept growing, the church opened the Marion Hillard Home for pregnant girls in Kamloops, British Columbia, in 1965. In 1955, the Presbyterians moved from crowded premises on Yorkville Avenue in downtown Toronto to a large estate that I will call Sterling, in Oakville, outside Toronto. The Pentecostal Benevolent Society opened its original Bethel Home in Scarborough in 1926, then built a new facility in the late 1950s.

But the leader of the rescue movement, at least in terms of numbers, was the Salvation Army. With its motto of "women and children first," the Army found a natural role for itself in this field. Its first Canadian home was in Toronto. Opened in 1887, the Home for Fallen Women was intended to rescue women from prostitution, redeem them, and make them respectable citizens. Its first home exclusively for pregnant, single women opened in 1905. The movement grew from there. Like the Sisters of Misericordia, the Army also opened hospitals across the country. Any city that had a Grace Hospital would also have one or more homes for unwed girls, often called Grace Haven (Regina, Montreal, and Hamilton) or Bethany (Saskatoon, Ottawa, Toronto, and Halifax). There were two Parkdales, in Calgary and Sydney, Nova Scotia. Other Army homes in Vancouver, Thunder Bay, St. John's, and London, Ontario, made up more than a dozen across the country.

The Maywood Home was built in 1959, after overcrowding forced the Army out of a "beautiful" Kitsilano residence it had used since 1906. Several flowering maywood trees on that property had given the home its name. According to a brief written history of Maywood, the name was put forward by "a lady who had been very helpful in suggesting furniture and draperies for some of the rooms – she was also able to suggest names of women who might be interested in beginning an auxiliary."

This anonymous woman's decorating talents were not in much evidence at the new Maywood when I arrived. It looked as plain as plain could be. I saw only blank walls and dull offices. In one of these I signed in. As was the custom in all the homes, I had to give up my last name for the length of my stay. Now I would just be Anne. My only other identifying feature was my due date.

Captain Elva Jolly wore a nurse's uniform that had been adapted for the home, with Army badges on the points of her starched white collar. Maywood was a new assignment for her. She had started out in the Army's B.C. headquarters, but her friendship with a Maywood officer and early visits to the home revealed a new vocation to her – social work with young girls. Today she says, "I came in July 1964, and let me tell you, the day I got my appointment to Maywood Home, I thought that I had died and gone to heaven. I really wanted to be appointed there. I really loved it." When I met her in 1967, Captain Jolly was twenty-eight, only eight years older than me. But her youth did not register on me, nor did the warmth and kindness that I felt when I talked to her recently. In 1967, I saw only the dark red-and-blue Army insignia she wore. I defined her by the roll call of rules she told me: up at seven, chapel every day, work schedules, mail times, day passes, visiting hours, and on and on.

I blankly followed her down the long corridor that divided the main floor, while she pointed out the rooms for various activities. The "library" turned out to be a single bookshelf. I noticed copies of *The Bobsey Twins* and *The Robe*, Lloyd C. Douglas's best-selling novel about early Christianity. In the schoolroom there were rows of wooden desks and chairs. Along the back and sides of the room stood rickety metal typing tables topped with clunky old Underwoods. I could hear my mother's voice: "A girl never has to worry about getting a job if she has her typing." In the common room, or lounge, I was introduced to several girls. I learned no home towns, no backgrounds, and, of course, no last names. "This is Shirley. She's due May 15. Now here's Linda. You're both due in late June."

I didn't really notice the girls, just their huge stomachs. Would I be like that? Was I like them now? They seemed so young, all baby faces and shy giggles. I had put so much stake in being twenty, no longer just a teenager, something more than just another "bad girl." But here I was no different from what I scornfully thought of as kids – girls I assumed were silly, too dumb to know better, and, in the language of the day, probably "cheap and common."

The depression that I had fought off for weeks was gaining on me as the tour continued upstairs. Off another long hallway were bedrooms with – at four to a room – enough spots for forty girls. Even so, Captain Jolly says, "We always had a waiting list of six weeks." But now I had a piece of luck. There was one room with only two beds. Captain Jolly must have sensed my reaction. She told me that I could be alone there if I liked, at least for now. I couldn't wait for her to leave so I could cry. But I didn't. I just sat on the bed and stared at the brown linoleum. I couldn't imagine how I was going to pass the next endless months.

—

Doing the research for this book has led me to a number of former Maywood girls. I've discovered that for some this

Salvation Army home was a sanctuary from unhappy families or staring schoolmates. Laura M., who had been coping for years with an alcoholic mother, says that for her it was a very secure, pleasant experience. She had a wonderful time there. Another girl, who had been out working, felt an enormous weight lifted. "I was grateful that I could go somewhere I didn't have to worry about paying rent," she says. "I would only have to pay three dollars a day for three meals a day and have a roof over my head. I didn't even look. I would have gone no matter what it was like."

Others were as lonely and frightened as I was. Now I wish I had been able to connect with some of them while I was there. Perhaps it was the timing. There were often older girls at Maywood. Had I gone a few months later, I would have met Ellen M., another twenty-year-old. She was new to Vancouver, too, having arrived a year earlier from Liverpool. Before Maywood, she'd soared on the popularity that automatically came in those days to anyone with a Mersey accent. Then she found herself pregnant with no support. She still remembers her first day at Maywood. "I will never forget it as long as I live," she says. "I was being shown my room, which was being shared by four people. The first young woman I laid eyes on was expecting twins. And I said, 'Oh my God, am I going to get that big?' It sort of dawned on me that I really was going to have a baby. And I felt – I will never forget the feeling – I really felt like I was in jail. I knew I had to hide away and stay there until it was all over. I looked at it like it was some type of a sentence. When I see people in movies being handcuffed and taken to jail, I think of that feeling I had. It was the feeling of not being free, not wanting to be there."

It's hard to know how well the homes were known in their towns or cities. In the Oakridge area of Vancouver, where Maywood was, everybody in the neighbourhood knew who came to the big house on the main street and why she was there. If the home had no space for a girl, she was often placed for light work with a local well-to-do family. Captain Jolly remembers, "We would have people call and say, 'Our girl has delivered, we would like another.' 'We sure liked this last girl and we would like another one just like her.'" One of my closest friends now, who grew up in the area, remembers how she and her friends used to pass by the house on the way to school, peering through the railings for a look at "one of them." But the location and the business of the homes were certainly not widely known. The Maywoods and Parkdales, the Bethanys and Grace Havens were not listed in telephone directories, and every house had the same rule: "The phone is only to be answered with a simple hello." Secrecy was the number-one priority.

Growing up, I had certainly heard of girls who "had to go away." A prolonged visit to a relative "to help out" or "to try a new school" was always a giveaway. Mononucleosis seemed epidemic among teenage girls. The long recovery time for "mono" and the risk of infection could hide a girl's condition for months, especially if it was the middle of the school year.

Nobody was fooled. But at the same time we didn't know exactly what happened to the girls who were there one day and gone the next. Though I was an active member of the Anglican Church, I never heard about Humewood or any of the three or four other places that a girl could go to in downtown Toronto. If I had seen Humewood, it might not have served as a caution. It was a lovely mansion, secluded among trees, with large flower and vegetable gardens. Even Maywood attracted some girls. One woman who lived nearby in the late 1950s as a young girl also recalls staring at the place in fascination. She saw girls who, she says, "looked like they were really having a good time, always laughing. I used to say, 'I'm going to go there when I grow up.' It was such a nice-looking place. I was about twelve

then. I was pretty naïve, I guess. I think maybe that's why my
father married me off early. At nineteen."

─

Its grand and graceful exterior often struck girls who saw the
Sterling Home in Oakville, Ontario, for the first time. This
Presbyterian home was where Karin went late in the fall of 1964.
My fantasy of a romantic mansion was a reality for her when she
and her family turned in to the circular driveway of the stone
and timber house originally built for a wealthy family in the
1920s. Even though the Sorensens had moved to a Rexdale
duplex after many years in their crowded apartment, Karin was
still impressed. "Oakville, which is now a built-up bedroom
community of Toronto, still had a lot of country in those days.
There were no other buildings nearby, and the home was set off
by large and beautifully kept grounds. There was still enough
fall colour to give it a kind of golden glow. I remember thinking
maybe this wouldn't be so bad. From the outside it looked like
one of those country inns, the kind they always advertise as a
romantic getaway from the pressures of the big city. If you take
out the 'romantic' and add a few months to the getaway, that's a
fairly accurate description of its purpose," she adds, "to get
away from the pressure."

Karin was relieved to get to Sterling. She had been warned of
the long waiting lists. Now she was almost six and a half months
pregnant. "Very pregnant," she emphasizes. "By the time I went
in I had spent several months hiding in the house, avoiding the
picture window that looked onto the street. From time to time, I
would be snuck out of the house and taken out of the city – for a
little airing, as it were – to some place like the Kitchener farmers'
market, where my parents thought it would be safe. My mother
was convinced that as long as nobody ever saw me pregnant,
no one could ever prove anything. I was pretty cut off from my

friends during this time." When Karin entered Sterling, her whole family shared her relief.

Karin's eyes widened when she walked into the front receiving room, where stilted visits were carried on with the few permitted visitors. Though the other girls called this room "the morgue," Karin was at first impressed by its formality, by the tapestry-covered rosewood chairs, the grand piano, and the attached conservatory. There were the same rules there as I had at Maywood, but the beauty of the home made them seem less restrictive to Karin. Upstairs, there was a new extension, where the girls were assigned to double and single rooms: bright, modern, and fairly cheery. "This did not feel like an institution," she says, "but a pretty place to hide if you had to hide." Karin settled in quickly, determined to make the best of it.

The other women I have met who went to Sterling all remember it as being lovely or beautiful. One says it was a classic example of late Victorian Arts and Crafts. Another remembers the fishpond with its Chinese footbridge, yet another the nearby apple orchard where she would go for walks.

Their memories of the woman who ran the home are more varied. Nobody seems to know just who Mrs. Hermann was – except that she was the boss. Karin did not have much to do with this middle-aged, no-nonsense German woman, with her grey hair drawn back in a severe bun, but her impression is of an intelligent, insightful person. Another Sterling girl who spent a lot of time with Mrs. Hermann said that she could really "zero in" on a girl and her problems. Karin thinks perhaps she had a background in social work. As there were no titles and uniforms there, she could have been anything from a glorified housekeeper to a trained psychologist. But she was not universally popular. One girl called her a Nazi, whose dictatorial style, despite the beauty of the home, made her feel like she was living in a barracks. Whatever her style, it seemed to terrify the two other women who worked in the house. Mrs. Stevenson (called Stevie) was a small, spry woman in her sixties who, Karin says, travelled at the speed of light. "We always knew it was she by the brisk clip-clop of her shoes down the hall. She was tremendously sweet and caring, but Mrs. Hermann frightened her and it was easy to ruffle her feathers." Karin also remembers the fifty-ish Mrs. Robinson, "Robbie," and the caretaker and his wife. He was quite cheerful, but the pinched demeanour of his wife reminded Karin and the others of Mrs. Danvers from *Rebecca*. "Though, thankfully," Karin says, "she didn't have tendencies to arson."

The more I learned about homes for unwed mothers in the postwar period, the more I came to see a real difference between the homes of the 1950s and the 1960s. In the early 1960s, many of the old homes proved too small for the number of girls needing to hide, and the Army and the Catholic Church both added new wings to many of their homes or looked for new facilities. As many other religious organizations felt the call to participate, they, too, opened shelters or renovated the ones they already had in order to meet the demand. The new homes tended to be more spacious, often with classrooms or craft rooms for the girls' "rehabilitation." Their atmosphere was cosier and less punitive. Sterling was one of these. Even Maywood, which had opened in the late 1950s, was more spacious and its rules less rigid than earlier Army homes. So girls who found themselves pregnant in the 1960s often had a better – if ultimately no less shameful – experience than those in the 1950s. Had Karin or I been hidden away a decade earlier, we would no doubt be remembering an even more oppressive experience.

The Bethel Pentecostal Home that Janet Roberts went to in Scarborough in 1957 was a world away from the grace and grandeur of Sterling. In those days Kennedy Road was not a busy thoroughfare, but more like a country road. The house she arrived at with her Aunt Vi was a red-brick, three-storey structure with a semicircular drive and large trees in the front; neighbouring houses and businesses were some distance away. Today it would be a renovator's dream Victorian farmhouse, but thirty years ago its featureless exterior held no appeal for Janet. The décor inside was just as Puritan. "Sparse, extremely sparse," Janet remembers. There were uncarpeted wood floors throughout, a large country kitchen downstairs, and big, plain bedrooms upstairs. In a few years this home would be too small and the Pentecostals would build a much larger residence elsewhere, but for now it held about a dozen girls, three or four to a room. Everybody ate together at the kitchen table. There was a yard outside where the girls could sit in good weather.

The Bethel Home does not seem to have had any trained staff. An older couple from the church ran it – a Mr. and Mrs. Harrison. They had a separate apartment upstairs and so did their son and his family. Janet remembers the senior Harrisons as kind people, but rigid about the rules. Once a girl had entered the home, she was not allowed to use the main door again until she left. The front part of the house, where the office was located, was also forbidden to the girls. They could go in the yard, but nowhere else, except for doctors' appointments. For those, they would be picked up at the side door and expected to get into and out of the house station wagon as quickly and unobtrusively as possible.

Janet, the children's nurse who had, in effect, been turned out by the relatives who had initially welcomed her to Canada so warmly, won't use the word home to describe Bethel. It was, she says, "a place where you went to get away from your own home so nobody would know you were pregnant. There were girls there as old as thirty and as young as thirteen. A lot of them came from out of town, places like Wiarton and Sarnia. You could come here and have it quietly and go back to your family. It was just a place to stay. I guess it was okay for me at the time because I had no place else to turn. I didn't know anybody or anything."

Janet had done what she needed to do: she'd found a place to hide. Because she was new in the country she didn't have to figure out an elaborate cover story. If anyone asked, her aunt and uncle would just say that she had gone to visit a friend or to the States for a trip. She disappeared so well that nobody even knew she was missing.

Like the circles in Dante's Inferno, there is a kind of descending order of homes. If Janet found Bethel sparse in 1957, it was still better than what many girls in other homes were experiencing at about the same time. It seems fashionable to find fault with the Catholic Church these days, and I am wary of easy verdicts. For the most part, all these institutions, whatever their faiths, were doing what they felt they had to for young girls in trouble. They saved many of them from far worse fates. But the stories I kept hearing about the Misericordia homes in the 1950s make it difficult not to pass some kind of judgement because of the cold and unfeeling attitude so many girls say they encountered. From some of these Sisters of Mercy, that quality seems to have been rather strained indeed.

Fourteen-year-old Loretta had been in the Catholic system since she was sent to convent school at age eight. After she was raped, when she was made a ward of the court, she "served time," as she puts it, at the Good Shepherd reform school. A few months later, without any explanation, she was shipped to yet another institution, the Misericordia Home for Girls in Edmonton.

The Misericordia Hospital had been built in various stages since the Sisters first arrived in Edmonton in 1900. It faced onto

111th Street, just a couple of blocks west of Jasper Avenue, where the Edmonton General Hospital is today. By the time Loretta arrived in 1956, it was, at least to a big-eyed, frightened little girl, a massive complex. Loretta wasn't allowed to enter through the impressive front doors. Like all the girls, she was taken around the back, to a separate building where she would be hidden from those coming and going through the main entrance of the hospital. The home was in the original power plant and laundry for the hospital, and the ground floor was still used twenty-four hours a day for washing and drying the hospital linen. The huge, old steel boiler went non-stop, and its cracks and whistles could be heard up on the second floor where the girls were kept. The heat from the laundry also seeped through the floor, and it was boiling hot up there most of the time. There were no separate bedrooms, just two long dormitories on either side of the nun's station, each lined with ten or twelve army cots. The floors were bare battleship linoleum and the walls institutional green. Each girl had a small table but no closet. What little she brought was stored under her bed.

Loretta put her things away and then sat on her bed, wondering what to do next. She was nervous and couldn't stay still, and she made her first mistake when she peeked out the window beside her. A nun rushed over from nowhere and pulled her roughly away. "We weren't allowed to open the curtains of the little windows. We faced onto a courtyard in the middle of the hospital, and we were not to impose upon other people who would see our pregnant bellies." Loretta had just learned rule number one, and there would be many more to come. Her first day was a series of psychic shocks. They were administered in the name of her protection and rehabilitation, but they felt like punishments.

The issue of her name came next, and Loretta was left with nothing of her own. She had to give up not only her last name –

that was standard in every home – but at the Misericordia the rule in 1956 was no real first names, either. Loretta was told she would be Rose – just Rose – for the rest of her stay. That would be her only identification on her medical file, too. Her last name would appear nowhere. "We could not use our real name or talk about our family. You were a nonentity there. They gave me no choice of what my name would be."

Loretta couldn't understand why she had to be Rose now and why she wasn't supposed to tell any of the other girls where she came from, or anything else about herself. The justification that it was for her own protection was just mystifying. She felt then and still feels now that whatever the intention, the spirit of the rule was demeaning and destructive, part of a calculated erosion of her self-respect.

The nuns wanted her "true" character to be made clear to Loretta as quickly as possible. After getting her new name, she was taken to see the hospital priest. Perhaps his compassion was exhausted that day by the patients he had visited in the wards, for he had none for the trembling girl who approached him. "I was Roman Catholic and I had Indian blood in me," Loretta says. "The priest told me I would burn in hell, that I was like an animal. He told me that there were convents I could enter because no man would want me. I tried to tell him what had happened. He told me not to make it worse by lying. I could go and do penance at a convent so that I could save my own soul, because there was no good RC man who would want me. I could somehow compensate and maybe save my own soul by doing this." If the priest's point was to terrify Loretta, he did his job well. From then on she was scared of the priests and the nuns there. "I called them the dark people."

But there was one exception, perhaps the one that has made it possible for Loretta to tell her story today without the bitterness she could easily justify. After her encounter with the priest, Loretta was taken to Sister Frances Cabrini. When Loretta tried to explain how badly she felt, she found a listener in Sister Frances. All the girls that I have spoken to from this Misericordia home remember Sister Frances with the same enormous respect and affection as Loretta does. "Sister Frances was in charge. She was wonderful, and we all liked her. She had more compassion in her eyes than anyone I have ever known in my life."

Sister Frances had just come the year before to the Misericordia's Edmonton home as its new director. Like Captain Jolly at the Salvation Army, she had chosen to work with young girls. Today, she still radiates the warmth and joy that attracted and consoled Loretta. She described to me the spiritual journey that took her as the young Sister Frances to the girls in Edmonton: "I am not sure where that came from in my life. I was the only girl at home. I wanted very much to give love, and to have love, and to have children. And I thought that if I married I might have two or three or five. But if I could work with children who don't have parents, or mothers who need to talk to somebody, maybe my maternal instinct would come out more. And so that's why I joined the order. It took a long time to find an order that was doing this. I was an American, and in the States I just couldn't find anything. I came to Montreal for a year as a boarder and I discovered this community, and it hit me like a brick. I thought, This is what I want. This is what I am looking for. I think that with the girls at the Miséricorde I was really – I felt really – like a real woman. They helped to bring out the woman in me, and the mother in me."

Sister Frances had been sent to Edmonton in 1955 with a request from her superiors to establish another home. The building she had to work with, she admits, was poor. "It was not – how shall I say? – cosy." She knew it was too hot and crowded, with no room for privacy or recreation. The girls had to go outside and across the courtyard for their meals, even in the coldest Edmonton weather. But a new building would take a lot of money. She was also concerned about some of the rules, such as the name change. For medical reasons she thought a girl's real name should be on file. But rules are hard to change. Not until after Loretta's stay was Sister Frances able to introduce some of her ideas. Her new home, Pineview, did not open until 1963. In the meantime, she did her best to share the gift she believed her order stood for. She was, as far as the circumstances allowed, a true sister of mercy.

Not all the girls at the Misericordia homes or other Catholic shelters were treated as harshly as Loretta was by her "dark people." Marg B., a devout Catholic who became another "Rose" during her stay at the Sundale Home in Chatham, Ontario, says that the Ursiline nuns were kind and caring. "Their hearts were nothing but good," she says. "I got so much comfort, solace, and support there. You could hardly carry on your former lifestyle and look God in the face." In Winnipeg in 1956, Audrey T., also Catholic, found the Misericordia plain, secretive, and distant, but not cruel. "It was impersonal," she says. "We were hidden away in this house. We ate and we slept, and we this and we that, but there wasn't much in the way of instruction of any kind. We were treated with toleration and judgement. We had sing-alongs, and we'd get together in the common room. One of the Sisters would play the organ. But there was nothing said. It was sort of a conspiracy of silence. I had the feeling years later that a distance was encouraged. Yet no one was unkind or miserable or judgemental to your face. It was all subtle. You know how nuns are. They're condescending and patronizing. For instance, treating us as if we had no brains, and that through our own lack of intelligence we had done the unspeakable and were totally responsible."

Wherever they were, everyone remembers losing their names. Where they were allowed to keep their first names, if there was more than one Cathy or Linda or Carol, they would be numbered. One woman I talked to still remembers herself as Cathy 4. The denial of a girl's family name was a rule in all the homes through the 1950s and 1960s. Anonymity was always explained as being for the girls' protection. They were at these homes for privacy from a stigmatizing society. They didn't want anyone outside or in to know who they were or where they had come from. But these sound more like rationalizations than reasons – justifications that confuse wants and needs. The girls certainly needed protection from a judgemental society, but they hardly wanted to lose half their identity. If the strategy protected anyone it was not the girls, but the families that had banished them.

The Sisters of the Misericordia had always insisted on changing each girl's name. In a paper sociologist Andrée Lévesque wrote for the Canadian Historical Association about single mothers at the Montreal Misericordia Home in the 1930s, she explains how chastening a girl's new identity was meant to be: "The first step, upon registration, was to receive an imposed name from an existing bank of names. The names were not ordinary ones but highly unusual and sometimes conveyed a meaning, such as Humiliane or Fructeuse! The names were assigned in alphabetical order and when the list was exhausted, after many months, the process started over again." A girl's depersonalizing was confirmed when she had to buy a two-dollar uniform. From the moment of registration until her departure, the *repentante*, or penitent, as she was known, was shut off from the world – and from her own identity.

Twenty years after the era that Andrée Lévesque describes, Marie Benoit stood shivering in front of La Miséricorde on a dry, chilly spring day, clutching the paper grocery bag she had packed with a few borrowed clothes. Only the neighbour who had given her bus fare knew where she was. Some changes had occurred inside the big stone edifice on St-Hubert just south of what was then Dorchester Street since the 1930s. Uniforms were not required after 1946, and Marie would not be named Fruitful or Humility. By the late 1940s, as another Quebec sociologist has written, "the sisters began to notice a change in attitude of the *filles-mères* who had in the past accepted their fate. The nuns who worked in the Quebec hospital declared that the modern young girls displayed a strong desire for freedom, independence and defiance. 'They are particular about the food and living arrangements, hate to work and are against being forced to stay. In short, the *filles-mères* do not accept their fate with the resignation of yesteryear.' "

Marie was still terrified. Pregnancy wasn't a crime, but she felt as guilty as if she had handcuffs on. La Miséricorde had always sounded like a prison to her, and now that she was staring at it from across the street, it looked like one. "It takes in a whole block. It is really impressive when you see it. It is sort of scary because I grew up with so many whispers about what happened to girls at La Miséricorde, and those big buildings always made me afraid. I felt like I was going into jail."

Once inside, Marie found the building no more comforting. "It was really very cold. Huge, high ceilings. It felt like it was all stone, you know. I'm sure it wasn't, not inside, but it just felt cold." The way she lost her last name was just as chilly an experience. "This nun came to greet me and she said, 'Sit down. What is your name?' I told her my name, and she looked at me and said, 'This is the last time you are going to use this name in this place.' I said, 'What do you mean?' She said, 'While you are in here you are not to speak to anybody about who you are, where you come from, what you do, you have to use a fictitious name.' This was all new for me. Had I known, I probably would have been able to prepare a name, you know, that would have meant something to somebody after. But I was stunned. I guess I wasn't talking, so she said, 'Take the phone book.' There was a phone book really neatly placed, like it was used a lot. And she said, 'Pick up the phone book and pick a name.' I opened the phone book and the name, I guess I didn't open it very much, it was in the B section, Brossard. She said, 'Well, do you want to keep your first name?' 'Can I?' 'Yes, you can, but don't tell anybody it is your real name.' My name became Brossard. 'Everything you say,' she said, 'everything you do, has to be under that name, and you remember that. Now you go to this floor.' And that was it."

Marie could keep her first name only if she pretended it wasn't hers. This self-denial stunned her. Brossard was the name of a place on the south shore that she had heard about. So, now, for some unfathomable reason, she was named after a town. "I felt like I was somebody else. I felt like I had really lost my identity, right there and then, in that room."

The nun didn't accompany Marie to her room, she just directed her to the elevator and told her to press the button for the third floor. Soon Marie discovered one thing that hadn't changed from the old days. Girls who could pay more were treated differently at La Miséricorde. They lived on another floor, where they each had a private room. For the length of their stay, they would be veiled and kept away from the other girls in the crowded third-floor dormitories. Marie didn't have that kind of money.

No one greeted her as she got off the elevator. She had to find her own way to one of the dorms. Perhaps all the Misericordia homes were built from the same blueprint, because Marie's room was almost exactly the same as Loretta's. Long and bare with a dozen or more beds perpendicular to the walls. "There was a cupboard, a shared cupboard, where they had some maternity clothes you could borrow. And there were drawers beside your bed. But there wasn't room for much. I guess that is why they told you not to bring very much. The room was just spotless. It smelled clean. Nuns' places, that's one thing to give them, everything is so clean. Spotless. But they don't do it themselves. I remember a bathroom that was so clean that it was cold. The only thing that I remember vividly was how cold it was. But there was something warm. Just because we were all in the same boat, there was some warm feeling between the girls."

In feeling the warmth of the other girls, Marie recognized on that very first afternoon what for many would be the true saving grace of the homes – the chance to be with others in the same boat. Although I avoided the other girls I met on my first day, others talk about feeling more at ease than they had in months. Sylvia J., who was in the Army's Grace Haven Montreal home in 1962, says, "I felt not quite so alone as I started to meet the other girls. I remember thinking, Well, there are a lot of people in the same situation." This alone could restore some of the self-respect the institution seemed bent on destroying. A year later, in the same home, Pat D., whose mother had made her stay at neighbours over Christmas so visiting family wouldn't guess her condition, felt the same relief at being among other girls with her problem. Despite all the efforts at secrecy, sometimes a girl would recognize someone she already knew. Laura M. at Maywood walked into the common room to see not just one but two girls she knew. One was a past Queen of Job's Daughter, one of the prettiest and most popular girls in her home town.

It's no surprise the girls gravitated to each other. There was no one else in the homes, except for nuns, Army officers, and church women. Even when the staff members were truly compassionate and practised their Christianity, the girls knew they were not "one of them." How could they be when, as late as the 1960s, girls at the Anglican Humewood House were referred to by staff – even if in a joking manner – as inmates. It was only the other girls who truly knew what you were going through. Although some girls did have close and long-lasting relationship with staff in the home – keeping in touch long after they had left and often thanking a nun or matron for all she had done – there was still a fundamental inequality at play. Sociologist Regina Kunzel points out in her study of American maternity homes, "One need not minimize the affection and respect that some unmarried mothers felt for maternity home workers to suggest that these relationships had other dimensions as well. To focus only on mutual respect is to flatten a much richer, more complex range of relations. Despite maternity home workers' assertions of equality, the undeniably unequal balance of power between unmarried mothers and the staff of the homes could not help but shape the relations between them. Although they could be harmonious and respectful, their relations were also often marked by tensions and conflict."

Linda Chalmers didn't gravitate to the other girls in the home she was sent to in Montreal. By the time she arrived, she was so confused and unhappy that she wanted neither to reach out nor to be touched by anyone else. At fifteen, she was a good deal younger than the other residents. "A varied and innocent lot," Linda says. "We were from all parts of the world: Ireland, Nova Scotia, and other regions of Canada." In retrospect she realizes they were probably just as confused as she was, but like mine at Maywood, Linda's response was to keep to herself. Still, where I judged the other girls, Linda simply collapsed into passivity and isolation.

In the last weeks, Linda had been pushed and pulled by her mother into situations she didn't want or understand. First it was the disastrous wedding trip and the humiliation of being jilted. Then she was abruptly put out to work as a maid. When she called home, crying that she couldn't stand being a servant to that cold, wealthy woman in Westmount, her mother hustled her off once again. Linda can remember where it was she was taken, and what it looked like, but nothing more.

"I don't know what it was called. I've tried and tried, but I can't remember," she says. "It was probably run by the Catholic Services, because it was through them I was sent there. I can't remember the staff, either. But they didn't look like nuns. They didn't wear habits.

"The home was on Stanley Street in a beautiful part of the city, near Peel, in the 'Golden Mile.' It was up on the hill, on the side of the mountain, just down from McGill. It looked like a lovely brownstone, New York style, but nicer. I remember a living room to the right. On Sundays, my mother would come to visit, and that's where we went and sat. Then there was a hallway with a staircase with a brass railing. I used to polish that railing every day. On the next level there were old people. I still don't know if they were ill or just living there; the place was shrouded in mystery. Then you went up to the top level, and that's where we were. There were about five or six of us in one big room. Just beds in the room. Beds and pregnant girls."

Beds and pregnant girls. That's a bald description, but it is all too accurate for these homes, no matter where they were. Girls often went to a home in another province to be really sure no one would know. This was particularly true in the Atlantic provinces. In Nova Scotia in the 1950s, when a girl went to Ontario, no matter what the reason given, everybody assumed it was to hide a pregnancy. In New Brunswick, if the girl's parents had any status or money, she would be bundled away on the night train from St. John to Montreal or points west. Prince Edward Island had two homes run by the Catholic and Protestant family services, but any girl who could manage it financially left for one of the homes in Halifax or Sydney.

In earlier days, many girls from the Maritimes and other parts of Canada and even the States found a place to stay at the once-flourishing Ideal Maternity Home in East Chester, Nova Scotia. They preferred this private home because it didn't make them feel guilty or try to redeem them. But that was not because of any progressive theories. The home was not interested in the fate of the girls. It was in the business of selling perfect babies. The less than perfect ones were neglected, and those that died were hastily and quietly buried in butterbox caskets out back. When news of this finally broke in the mid-1940s, the home was shut down. By the 1950s, only religious organizations offered unwed mothers a secret place to stay. In Halifax, there was the Catholic Home of the Guardian Angel. The Little Flower Institute was located in Little Bras d'Or, and in Sydney, the Salvation Army ran the Parkdale House.

There was not nearly as much choice for an unwed mother in Newfoundland. Although the Roman Catholic Church dominated religious life, the Salvation Army had the major role in rescue work. The Army's soldiers had first invaded the island in 1884, beginning a long and vigorous war against sin and corruption, attracting many converts, especially in the outports, with their evangelical fervour. But for the Army it was the city that was the great den of iniquity. By 1897, a home for unwed mothers, The Anchorage, was established at 26 Cook Street in St. John's. A Grace Hospital soon followed, and later a new home for girls, the Glenbrook Lodge.

Beth Holmes wasn't told about Glenbrook when she found herself in trouble. On a wintry March day in 1967, she went to 18 Wood Street, just a five-minute walk up from the harbour.

Molly Breen's was the middle of three attached, plain-fronted clapboard houses, the kind you see on Newfoundland postcards that are always painted bright colours. Molly's was a sunny yellow – just about the same colour as her hair. She wore it rolled up very neatly, and her clothes were always carefully pressed – Molly never liked to look sloppy – but there was nothing else formal about her. Beth can speak very tersely about many of the other people she had to deal with at that time – her dad, her boyfriend, the people from Social Services – but when she talks about Molly there are no reservations, only immense affection. "She just had this motherly face and she always wore a dress, something like the mother in the Waltons," she says. "I know that sounds silly, but that's what she was like. She was the mother I always wanted, that I always would have liked to have had. She was there for the girls, and she talked to us like we were her own daughters. She never put any of us down. We were just 'girls who had made a mistake' or who had 'got in trouble.' Those were her words."

Beth didn't pay to stay at Molly Breen's. The government gave Molly a weekly stipend for each girl, and she was licensed to house up to thirty at a time. But although it was often crowded, nobody who stayed there thought Molly was in it for the money. Some of the girls used to whisper that Molly had had a daughter and something had happened to her, but nobody really knew for sure how or why she started taking in girls. Her husband, Herb, was always around, a little man, a Mutt to her Jeff. Beth remembers him. "He would be sitting on the steps as we went back and forth up the stairs, to and from our rooms. He would pat the girls as they'd go by – I don't mean in a sexual way – or he'd say, 'How'ya doin', my ducky?' or something like that. He would just sit there. He was in his own little world."

This was 1967 and Molly was then in her mid-fifties – that meant she would be more than eighty, if she was still alive, at the time I started doing research. I couldn't locate any records that mentioned the house on Wood Street, and I never once expected to find Molly herself. But when I was in St. John's visiting Beth, we went to look at Molly's old place and we turned into detectives for an afternoon. No one was home at number 18, the people in the adjoining houses had only recently moved in, and the neighbourhood historian said he remembered a Breen family but nothing about any pregnant girls. Finally we hit paydirt with a woman who had lived across the street for forty years. "Molly Breen. Sure I remember Molly and all those girls," she told us. "I think she's still around. You could call her son, I think she lives with him now."

An hour later Molly Breen herself was telling us about how and why she had started taking in pregnant girls. Now eighty-five, she still has yellow hair, and she was dressed as neat as a pin. She was thrilled to talk to us about the old days. It was true she had lost a daughter as a little baby, but that was years before she had started to take in "her girls." In 1963, when she bought the house on Wood Street, she had already run several businesses, including a catering service and delicatessen downtown. But her husband, Herb, had just had an operation for brain cancer, which explains why the girls found him so vague, and Molly wanted to stay closer to home. Somebody told her about how many unmarried, pregnant girls needed a place to stay, and she opened her doors. She did get a Social Services stipend, but just as often, she says, "I'd give the girls that money back. I don't know how many times I did that."

That's what Molly was like – generous, warm, loving without judgement. Perhaps in old age she's become a bit confused – from the hard hug and smacking kisses that she gave both me and Beth, I wondered if she thought I, too, had stayed at Wood Street – but I know I wanted to collapse like a child into her embrace that day. And I could tell, just as Beth had said, that

Molly's had never been the kind of official love for the sinner that too often turned into rules and regulations. Beth didn't have to change her name. There were no limits to where the girls could or couldn't go except one: Molly always made sure they went to their regular checkups. There was no argument about that. "There was no such thing as you didn't want to go," Beth says. But that insistence sometimes got Molly herself into trouble. "She had us all overweight. I remember that very clearly. Every one of her girls, when we'd go for checkups, would be overweight. And I remember Social Services checking into her about that, because Social Services believed it wasn't good what she was doing to the girls in terms of stuffing us. But we loved it."

Food came up as a subject again and again among the women I talked to. It's not that they ever went hungry; some girls were eating the best meals they'd ever had. Marg B., who was at Sundale in Chatham, Ontario, says, "There were kids that moaned about the food, but I'd come out of Kraft Dinner and Coke. It was a delight." She had no difficulty when the nuns asked her to be "a positive influence and tell the others that the food was okay."

The complainers often objected that better food was being dished out to the matrons and supervisors at the homes. Pat D., who was at Grace Haven in Montreal, says, "Their meals were completely different from ours. We were eating hamburger and spaghetti, and melts, and things nobody liked. They were having roast potatoes and roast beef and stews and nice meals." A Maywood girl who served dinner to the officers in the Big House, a separate building from the girls' residence, used to look with envy at the meals she passed to them. Lelani D. at the Army's home in Calgary considered herself lucky because she used to wash dishes at the old people's home, where they had salt on the table. "I could finally get some flavour in my food," she says.

The girls at Molly's never complained about the food. In every other home you took what you got; at Molly's you ordered what you wanted. Molly was one of those great natural cooks, and she loved to feed her girls. Beth says, "We were all treated excellently. We had what we wanted to eat. And that was a big thing for me, coming from where I came from. In the evening she'd ask us what we wanted the next day – pies or whatever you liked. She had giant-sized cooking boilers on a big stove. She would be up all night making soup and cakes. And then she had these specialties – turkey pies, sausage rolls, molasses puddings. It was amazing."

—

So there we were in our new homes. Beth comforted at Molly Breen's, Linda at her nameless brownstone in Montreal, Marie and Loretta frightened by the nuns of La Miséricorde, Janet with her new Pentecostal family, Karin ensconced at Sterling, me at Maywood. Just seven of the thousands of girls who found themselves in an old house or a brick building wondering where they had ended up and what was to come. How we coped with the following months, of course, depended partly on us. An angry girl could find fault with the best of places, a desperate one might accept the harshest of conditions. But whether the home felt like a refuge or a prison depended not only on the girl's attitude, but also on the culture within and around these maternity homes and the ambivalence of society towards girls in trouble.

How the homes were run in the 1950s and 1960s reflected almost a century of changing ideas about what an unwed mother represented and how she should be treated. There is an often-told story in the States from the late nineteenth century about how Kate Waller Barrett, an early organizer of the Florence Crittendom homes for unwed mothers, came to do rescue work. One night a cold, wet young woman appeared on her doorstep with a fatherless child, seeking Barrett's husband, a minister. In one of those "there but for the grace of God go I" moments, Mrs. Barrett wondered what she would have done if she had loved a "bad" man instead of a "good" one. She was moved by this bond of sisterhood and angered by the injustice of the world that would dismiss her as a fallen woman.

It was this impulse of largely middle-class evangelical women, as Barrett put it, to "reach down and clasp the hand of a fallen sister" that led to the establishment of the earliest homes in Canada, such as Haven House and St. Mary's Infants Home in Toronto. But the purity of the intention cast its own dark shadow. In the very act of "reaching down," these same women were standing firm for their own moral order: reaffirming their superior station and protecting their world from those whose actions (sex outside wedlock) and its results (illegitimate children) could profoundly affect it. As the fallen woman was being embraced by sisterly and Christian love, she was being told how she could retain it: by changing herself. In the very act of singling her out for help, these well-meaning women strengthened and perpetuated the stigma of the unwed mother both in her own and the eyes of others. The privacy they offered became hiding, their help became her shame, their charity, punishment.

By the end of the First World War, the private groups of evangelical women had largely been replaced by missionary projects of organized churches, which took up the work in the same spirit of rescuing the fallen. They welcomed the girls with sympathy; they were "good girls" who had temporarily lost their way or who, because of "bad men," had "made a mistake." The homes gave them a place to hide while they rehabilitated and redeemed themselves.

"They were just girls who had made a mistake" is a phrase often repeated by staff of the churches' postwar homes. Molly

Breen said it, too, but with an important difference. Hers was not the patronizing attitude of the benevolent nor an attempt at spiritual deliverance. When the Salvation Army used the same language, it came with an agenda attached. As the brigadier of one home in the 1960s put it, "It wasn't the mistake but what a girl did with it that mattered." For the religious, there was always a soul to be saved for Jesus. In the loving but firm atmosphere they provided, a girl could see the light, be raised up, and be returned to the world. Grace was available, but it came with strings attached.

The joy of rescuing sinners undoubtedly motivated many to help their less fortunate sisters, but there was another and perhaps more common theological view of them. These girls had fallen, not just from their own naïveté, but from the evil inherent in every women. The serpent had tempted Eve, but she had tempted Adam. She was the fount of original sin. Historically, it was this demonization of women that informed and undermined much of the charitable Christian rescue work.

We only have to look at the punitive atmosphere in so many of the homes in the 1950s, and those in Quebec well into the 1960s, to confirm that view. The unwed mother, or *fille-mère*, was deemed to be less sinned against than sinner. Sociologist Andrée Lévesque points out, "Historians of Quebec have long been familiar with the central importance of the patriarchal family and women's role as mother within the home. What has received little attention has been the fate of those that defied the cultural norm and conceived out of wedlock. According to contemporary Catholic mores, such individuals undermined the social order and, through their transgressions, brought shame on themselves and their kin."

The callous taking away of names, the covered windows, even the bare dormitory rooms and plain iron beds express the churches' regard for these girls. They would keep them, for they had a mission to keep them, but warmly forgiving them was another matter. Lévesque goes on to say that girls at La Miséricorde in Montreal who truly wanted to redeem their innocence were encouraged to join the order of the Madelon, named after St. Mary Magdalen, and become oblates. The oblates did not have the strict discipline of the nuns – fasting was not required, for example – but shrouded in brown robes, they worked for the nuns, doing housework and sewing, and thus atoned for their sins. Between 1905 and 1964, more than a thousand *filles-mères* in Quebec "took the veil" in this manner. Many passed the rest of their lives inside the religious institution they had come to as desperate young women.

The new liberalism of the Roman Catholic Church after the Council of Vatican II in 1962–65 allowed a more sympathetic and embracing view of the unmarried mother. But how the girls were treated in all the homes in the 1960s was also affected by a very secular factor: the rise of the professional social worker.

American sociologist Regina Kunzel in her book *Fallen Women: Problem Girls* traces the effect of social work on the definition and treatment of the unwed mother. As the discipline developed from its volunteer beginnings in the early decades of the twentieth century into the professionalism of the postwar years, the old problem and its solutions came to be framed not in moral but in "scientific" terms. To the university-trained social workers, the girls were neither tainted angels nor hopeless sinners, but cases to be analysed in the context of the new social sciences. Morality and theology gave way to the new paradigms of sociology and psychology.

The sociologists saw the girls as a prime example of female deviance. The norm was for girls to date, to get married, and only then to have sex and get pregnant. Girls "in trouble" were not girls who lacked information about birth control or who may have been experimenting with sexuality. Rather, they were

acting out the female form of juvenile delinquency that so preoc-
cupied adults in the 1950s and 1960s. They were rebels without
a cause, not accidentally pregnant but initiates into a life of
wrongdoing. Harsh measures against them were well justified.
This is how the Canadian Welfare Council viewed the unmarried
mother in 1957: "Illegitimate pregnancy may be a sign of inability to meet satisfactorily the pressures and responsibilities of
adulthood. Like stealing, setting fires, and difficult behaviour in
school, it may be a symptom of a fundamental problem. And in
later life similar problems may result in, for example, alcoholism
or marital discord."

The psychologists took a more sympathetic view of the
girls' behaviour. As the early evangelicals had done, they saw "a
mistake." Where the church women had seen a sweet young
thing brutalized by a cad, however, the psychologists saw a girl
who acted out her private dilemmas in sexual indiscretion. For
them, the girl in trouble was a troubled girl. She was the girl
defined at the Out of Wedlock conference in 1964 as having a
deficient ego or unresolved Electra complex. Papers presented at
the conference variously described her as "psychically weak"
with a "strong need for a dependent relationship with a male
whose wishes had to be carried out at any cost." Her pregnancy
"may be an attempt or incidental attempt at resolving a
conflictual life situation." The most influential theorists of the
time came up with lists of psychological motivations to explain
unwed pregnancy. In 1945, psychiatrist Helen Deutsch published a book that listed five such unconscious factors: "her need
for affection and search for tenderness, her lack of maturity, her
weakness of self, and the case of adolescence to which sexual
activity was an act of rebellion and independence in the face of
their mother." Nine years later, in her book *Out of Wedlock*, the
influential psychologist Léontine Young reduced the hazards to

four: a dominating mother, a dominating father, an incapability to communicate, and a need for "autopunition."

Although social workers did not work directly in the homes until the very late 1960s, by the start of the decade, most provincial governments were insisting a caseworker be attached to every girl, primarily for the process of adoption. With their secular dogmas, these outside experts threatened the missionary-style work of the homes. But gradually as governments made more substantial financial contributions, and wanted a greater say, the "scientific" theories took hold. Staff members in the homes often took social-work courses themselves, even degrees. But the religiously motivated did not capitulate completely to the secular model. They could pick from the various theories to fit their institution's traditions and values. Those who saw a girl as a sinner had their view confirmed by the model of the juvenile delinquent. She should be punished for her own good. For the more sympathetic, the psychologists' "troubled girl" theory justified their model of redemptive love and acceptance.

For both schools of thought, the homes were not simply a place for the girls to hide. Whether a sinner or a victim, a girl could use her time in the home to find her way back to social acceptance and normalcy. By knowing and following the rules while she was there, she might either repent or come to understand the price of non-conformist individualism. But whichever road she was led down, she had work to do.

# 3

# *Earning Your Keep*

*"Work assignments are light, therapeutic and assigned with consideration of the girls' physical condition. Duties are changed frequently and there is no indication of any girl being overworked."*

*"All Homes are under religious auspices, and religion plays an important role in each Home, although no program is dominated by excessive religious influences. Attendance at religious services is voluntary, but in most cases the girls are encouraged to attend."*

– Report on Maternity Homes in Metropolitan Toronto, 1960

On my first morning at the Maywood Home for Girls the wake-up call came far too early. I had been living on my own for two years, setting my own schedule, which for me meant late nights and late days – not getting up at what felt like the crack of dawn. Also, sharing a bathroom in a boarding house was one thing, but here thirty or forty of us were herded into one communal bathroom. With our big bellies we probably did look like cows at a water hole, edging each other out to get at the line of sinks and toilet stalls. I hated it.

Then came more herding as we clomped downstairs for breakfast. We lined up with our pastel Melmac plates and snaked through the kitchen and into the dining room, where we sat at round tables in groups of eight and ten. The food was plentiful enough and undoubtedly nutritious, but it only made me all the more disheartened. Living by myself, I could gorge on brown-sugar sandwiches for breakfast if I wanted. But this wasn't my home, and there were too many of us for any to be indulged. We weren't "normal" pregnant women who could eat whatever we fancied in the middle of the night, but wayward girls fed three meals a day, strictly by the Canada food rules. I wonder now, as I recall all of us spooning down our porridge and dutifully drinking our milk, if we weren't, in some sense, producers at a baby farm. Weren't we being fed this careful balance of vitamins and minerals to produce healthy children for anxious customers, out there somewhere waiting for their new perfect child to be delivered?

One girl at a Salvation Army home in Montreal remembers her first day as "learning all the rules and regulations and what we were supposed to do to earn our keep." I soon learned this lesson, too. The first duty was chapel – fifteen minutes every morning, and compulsory. For this we were shepherded down to the basement. If there was anything I was prepared for, it was the Army's "religious stuff." I expected fire and brimstone or at least some authentic Major Barbara passion. But the service was short and simple – a Bible reading, a prayer, and a hymn. I can easily daydream my way through this, I thought.

I had more difficulty with the work we were expected to do. After chapel, we trooped back to the main floor and lined up for our chores. Perhaps it is unfair to label these chores as work, as they were not hard. But the cooking and cleaning had to be done. That's what we did all morning. Each girl was given her assignment. Illness was the only excuse not to work. As a new girl, I was on bathroom duty.

Equipped with scrub brush, mop, and pail, I went back upstairs. Getting up early had been hard, breakfast grim, and chapel dispiriting, and now as I stood alone in that huge white room, looking at all the toilets and sinks I had to swab out, I felt small and humiliated. I had sinned, and now I was being made to pay. I had no courage to rebel, only the energy to feel sickened by my situation. I just wanted all of it to be over.

It is difficult to explain – and I can't justify – the overwhelming depression and resentment I felt. Was I just lazy? A middle-class princess whose mother had usually picked up after her? There certainly was an economic reason for these morning chores. The Salvation Army wasn't a wealthy organization; there were a lot of girls to be taken care of. Why shouldn't we help clean and cook for ourselves? But I still felt ashamed and somehow disgraced.

Historically, the work the girls did at maternity homes always had a purpose beyond its practicality, and, in fact, the economic benefits to the home are rarely mentioned in the literature of the time. Rather, the emphasis is on the redemptive and rehabilitative effects of "light work" on the girls. The rules, regulations, and work requirements (shown opposite), which were laid out at the turn of the century for a Salvation Army home, give some idea of how the environment of a home was supposed to foster responsibility and respectability.

In those Victorian times, conformity to the ideal included the wearing of any questionable article of female adornment. "Girls must lay aside flowers, feathers, bangs and bustles while in the Home." By the 1950s and 1960s, when I and the others in this book found ourselves in maternity homes, accessories were no longer the problem. But there were new rules about behaviour and dress, which had a strong ring of the old. In my time,

# RULES AND REGULATIONS

— of —

## Rescue Homes.

There are no cast-iron rules to ensure the general good conduct and industry of the inmates of the Army homes, and the transcending power is love – sisterly, Christ-like love.

While this is the case, there are a few simple regulations which are necessary to the maintenance of unity, good-will and discipline. Below is appended a brief outline of these rules:

### RULES FOR HOME

| | |
|---|---|
| Rise at 6 a.m. | Open-air recess till 1.30 p.m. |
| Breakfast at 7 a.m. | All hands in workroom, 1.30 p.m. |
| Housework till 9.30 a.m. | First bell for supper, 5.15 p.m. |
| Prayers from 9.30 to 10 a.m. | Supper at 5.50 p.m. |
| All hands in workroom at 10 a.m. | Night school or meeting, 6.30 p.m. |
| First bell for dinner, 12.15 p.m. | Prayers from 8 to 8.30 p.m. |
| Dinner from 12.30 till 1 p.m. | Retire to bed, 8.30 p.m. |

#### Every Order must be Punctually Obeyed.

Girls must be willing to do such work as the Officers appoint cheerfully.

Girls must render willing obedience to their Officers.

Girls must lay aside flowers, feathers, bangs and bustles while in the Home.

Girls must be neat and clean in their person and habits.

No tobacco must be brought into the Home, neither snuffing nor chewing.

Girls must address their Officers respectfully, always using their titles.

No allusion must be made to former life, neither bad language used.

No talking allowed in bedrooms.

No girl allowed to go to her bedroom during the daytime.

Every girl is expected to stay six months.

Girls infringing these rules are subject to dismissal.

By order,

THE FIELD COMMISSIONER.

anyone who defied the "no shorts, no short skirts" dress code was deemed "unladylike"; complainers were considered rebels. In many ways, the daily regimen, the duties, and the general demeanour expected were not much different from those at the turn of the century. Prudence Mors Rains, now a sociologist at McGill University, published a study in 1971 of several homes in the States that considered themselves to be progressive. Even in those the themes of responsibility and respectability were paramount. The girls were in a home because they had forgotten, or perhaps had never learned, basic moral and social values. One of the ways to prove to the staff and to themselves that they were essentially good girls who had made a mistake was by following all orders and regulations without complaint or objection. An Army mission statement from 1954 makes this clear:

> The best possible medical and nursing care, plus religious and moral training are offered to the expectant mother. With wise counsel and guidance constantly being imparted by the officers on the staff, many of the girls leave our home with renewed hope and courage, returning to their family and community life better equipped morally and spiritually to take their place as useful members of society.

This passage gives a telling description of how those who sponsored the homes regarded their charges. If we were to be "better equipped morally and spiritually" when we left the home, then we obviously were deficient in those qualities when we came in. That was why we had allowed ourselves to get pregnant in the first place. At the home we could learn new behaviour that would prevent us from ever making such a mistake again. Within the protection of its secluded and secret environment, we could practise being "good girls."

One thing we could practise in the home was work – domestic work. Chores could teach a girl discipline and prepare her for her future married life, if she were successfully reconstructed. Captain Jolly at Maywood put it this way: "We had chapel. Then we went to our work sections. Some dusted, some vacuumed, some helped peel the veggies – none of it was very hard. But we were trying to encourage social interaction. Some kids didn't know. I remember asking one youngster to peel the Brussels sprouts, and she peeled all the leaves off them. We tried to expose them to all kinds of vegetables and give them ideas for when they became homemakers."

The obvious irony in this went unnoticed. In being pregnant we had taken on the most important of all the homemaker's functions. But we were not going to be able to use our new skills on our child. That would be postponed until some later, legitimate baby.

Not everyone I have talked with felt that the rules and work were punitive. Girls who had already slaved in wage homes found the duties required of them at the home a relief. Pat D., who was at Grace Haven in Montreal, doesn't understand my bitterness at being assigned to the bathroom detail. "It really didn't bother me at all," she says, "because it was so easy compared to working for the family I had been placed with originally. [At the home] we would do the chores, the vacuuming, clean the washrooms, change all the beds. Yes, it was like penance, but, on the other hand, if you didn't have that to do, what would you have done? Roamed the streets all day?" Girls who had come from particularly difficult situations at home often welcomed the discipline and order. One woman who had been in a home in Winnipeg said, "I looked at the Salvation Army people as orderly and functioning and having some kind of stability because at home I never knew what was coming out of left field."

Others felt the shame that I did. Across the street from Maywood at the Our Lady of Mercy Home, Pam G. initially volunteered for the garbage detail, but when her correspondence courses arrived she wanted to concentrate on schoolwork. When she asked to be let off her duties, the nun in charge asked Pam if she thought she was "too good for this kind of work." Jean D. was at the United Church home in Burnaby, British Columbia. She says, "I remember being scoffed at for not understanding the certain order that you did stuff. Like dusting before you vacuum. They were very picky-picky about a lot of stuff. You were definitely there like it was a punishment. And you should be darn thankful that you had this wonderful place to go to."

Perhaps it was the older girls, like me, who found this work demeaning. We had been testing out adult life in many ways – not just sexually. We had been out working or had left home for university. But now that we had made our mistake, we had lost our grown-up status. As Ellen M., the Liverpool girl at Maywood, puts it, "I felt treated like a child. It's like your mom says you're grounded and you're going to have to wash the kitchen floor for a week because you've been naughty. That kind of a feeling. For me, it wasn't done with good will. It was done because I felt I had to do it. It was the least that I could do."

In order to fulfil the second part of the Army's mission – to equip us better morally and spiritually – work was augmented by prayer. At Maywood, besides daily chapel, there was a weekly Thursday-night service. The pressure to convert was quite open in the 1950s. Audrey M., who was at Homeside in Winnipeg in 1956, remembers the Army's mercy seat being placed at the front of the chapel for any girl who wanted to come forward to kneel and be blessed and prayed over. By 1967, the weekly chapel meetings at Maywood were voluntary. The Army even tried to bring in ministers from other faiths.

Each girl had a limit to what she could take. For me, the limit was the work, not religion. Despite my Anglican upbringing and a deep interest in questions of faith, I had not been convinced by any theology I had encountered. I did not think that God, as portrayed in any of the descriptions I'd heard so far, had much to offer in my situation. I would have preferred more practical solutions such as birth-control information. For many others, the hymns and sermons and prayers only added to the load of guilt they were already carrying. One woman who was at Maywood a year before me says, "That was when I learned all the hymns that I didn't know. I'll always remember the one about walking in the garden alone when the dew is still on the roses and think of how in the chapel I always felt like a sinner. The people who ran that home were very good Christians, but it was real clear to me that I was a bad girl and they were good. They never really said that. But I felt treated like a bad girl, like a child."

Yet the staff in the homes did not see themselves as pushing religion, and the fact that some girls felt they had been treated as sinners might come as a surprise to the officers. Captain Jolly believes her Christian views underlaid, not overlaid, her actions. "I tried to marry my belief to my behaviour. I believed in what we were doing, and I believed that we should not push religion down the kids' throats. It was available. It was part of our program. But we never tried to get people to join the Salvation Army. We just wanted to tell them in their hour of need that the Salvation Army believed in God, and that we were there if they were interested in pursuing that."

Even when religion was not pushed, the deep faith of those who ran most of the homes was obvious. It had led them to this missionary work. The girls would intuitively know that their greatest success in the home – the way they could win the most approval – would be to aspire to some kind of spiritual transformation. In an Army pamphlet published a few years ago, Captain Jolly reported how a former resident had called to say she was now a Christian. "Can you imagine the excitement I experienced when I heard Linda's voice . . . ," Jolly wrote. "Linda wanted to share her good news. She is now a Christian, sings in a choir and teaches a Bible class. 'New life' in Christ was hers."

A conversion was always the occasion for rejoicing among the staff. An anonymous nun who kept a diary while she worked at St. Mary's Infants Home in Toronto tells us of one conversion. Among the mundane worries about lack of space and the price of butter are the moments of transcendence that made it all worthwhile for her. These are excerpts from entries in the winter of 1955:

January 12. Today we admitted a Japanese girl, a convert for two years. She was a pianist. Our hope was that she would be able to play the organ at the chapel for us. We had 6 to 8 requests for admissions. Because of lack of space, we were forced to delay their admission too late. We received our new typewriter today.

February 19. Sr. Marie Madeleine had the consolation of having a girl convert to our faith. This girl was born of Catholic parents but raised by a Protestant family. She asked for instructions. The chaplain, Father Firth, did everything to enlighten her. He taught her catechism and baptized her and her child. The next day, the Divine Host came to dwell in the heart of this newly baptized child.

February 20. Our new convert was filled with happiness. She was presented with a cake, best wishes and a few gifts. May this happiness radiate on all her existence. This was what we asked the Blessed Virgin for. The girls sang for her at mass.

March 2. Following our request to the government, to benefit from the reduction in price for the surplus butter, we received the authorization to buy some at 21 cents a pound.

March 20. The television was out of order once more.

It was not just the Roman Catholics or the Salvation Army whose mission was to bring the girls back to God and good Christian ways. The United Church called its shelters Redemptive Homes until well into the 1950s, and in its annual reports a list of "results" was headed by a carefully tabulated number of those who had made "professions of faith." The prayer for the Anglican Humewood House said, "God grant us that the House may be a place of rest and recovery of body and spirit and that all who use it may be led onwards from grace to grace until they come to thine everlasting Kingdom. The work is first and always spiritual, recognizing the only safeguard and the only natural and happy life is the knowledge and love of God and the consequent living in His presence." Even the secular authorities saw religious practice as a significant route to comfort and illumination. A report from 1960 on Metropolitan Toronto maternity homes describes the value of an interview with a chaplain: "The role is an important one and he can be most influential in rehabilitating an unmarried mother providing he is genuinely interested, sympathetic, non-judgmental and accepts the individual girl without condoning her unacceptable behaviour."

At Sterling in Oakville, Karin Sorensen felt neither the mortification of work nor the pressure to pray. She felt relief. "At least you could breathe there – literally," she says. Like the girl who'd worn two girdles before she had found a hiding place, Karin had spent so many months holding her stomach in that she felt an exhilarating freedom in her first days at the home. As for the chores and the "churchiness," she found them both almost laughable. After making sure that life during the first six months of her pregnancy was as normal as possible, she wasn't about to take any of the guilt or salvation too seriously. Life at the home, she says, "was regimented with chores – or studies, if you could do some correspondence courses. We even had to fold bandages a few times a week, though God only knows what for. We had weekly meetings with a minister. I have no recollection of what was discussed, just that they were compulsory and breathtakingly boring."

One of the social-work theories of the day held that the unwed mother's plight was not an issue of morality but of personality and values. She lacked the self-respect that would ensure her acceptance of, and compliance with, prevailing social mores. Accordingly, by doing chores she would learn not just how to clean or do laundry but, more important, how to take responsibility and carry out a task. There would be even more benefits if she could see herself as accomplished and successful. To this end, many homes had various special roles the girls could be elected or appointed to, such as social convenor or "senior girl." At Sterling, team leaders were picked for the various household tasks. Karin was elevated to one of these positions. "Apparently," she recalls dryly, "I showed leadership ability."

Karin was not particularly impressed by her new job, but it did bring one great benefit. The team leaders met daily to discuss their plans. This was where Karin met Judy Graham and formed the friendship that would be the best part of her stay at Sterling.

On the surface they seemed an unlikely pair. Karin was eighteen and had just completed high school. She was easygoing. Her family had not rejected her because of her pregnancy. On the contrary, her parents felt sharply the cruelty and hypocrisy of a society that insisted their daughter be hidden away. Though it was not their first choice, they went along with the convention of hiding their daughter rather than risk the opprobrium that would have been heaped on her if she had remained at home. But the secrecy and the shame were, they thought, harsh and unusual punishments. As Karin's mother told me, "At that time these girls were considered 'bad girls' or 'sluts.' Most of them weren't, and it was heartbreaking for parents to have to put away their daughters."

Judy Graham's parents didn't share the Sorensens' critical view of contemporary mores. They were a proper couple, originally from England, her father a prosperous Kingston businessman, her mother an accomplished homemaker. They had prided themselves on their perfect children, and had not recovered from the shock of what Judy had done to them. She certainly looked the model daughter. With her corn-coloured hair, styled in a shoulder-length pageboy, she looked like the Breck Girl in the shampoo ads. Judy had been a high-school cheerleader – that *ne plus ultra* sign of success – and in 1964 she was in second year at Queen's University. But she didn't have the inner confidence that her immaculate exterior suggested. Underneath that perfect shell was a girl who could think for herself and who had a healthy streak of independence, but these were qualities that hadn't yet been given much exercise. Judy judged herself harshly by the rigorous moral standards she had absorbed at home and at church. She felt the shame of her pregnancy deeply. She had been told she was a sinner, and had no reason to believe otherwise. In bouncy, extroverted Karin, Judy found the kind of girl perhaps she secretly wanted to be, or really was. She was immediately attracted to Karin's confident, free spirit and wanted to be friends with this girl who, right away, made her feel she might not be so bad after all. "We were in the kitchen working, and Karin made a mistake or something and said, 'Oh fuck' and then laughed," Judy remembers. "I'd never said the F-word before, and here was somebody who was really neat and wasn't afraid to say something like that. I liked her from that moment on. We just connected. It was sort of cool, to me, to meet someone like Karin in that goody-goody place."

Today, both Judy and Karin independently use the same phrase to describe their friendship: "We made it fun for each other." Together, the two girls found they could cope at Sterling. In Karin, Judy found the first person who didn't think either of them had done anything wrong, and who seemed to think, at least on the surface, that the place they were in now, with its middle-aged biddies fussing over rules and regulations, was all a bit silly. In Judy, Karin found somebody who would laugh with her. "My need was to deny, and joke," she says. "And Judy would join in with me and support me. What we did was support each other in our odd ways of dealing with it all. Does that make sense?"

They found a fine focus for their humour in the religious part of Sterling's program. The home didn't have a daily chapel service, but a pastor came in once a week for a spiritual chat with the girls. Karin and Judy could barely control themselves on those Thursday evenings. The dough-faced minister, who was trying to instil a sense of virtue in this group of wayward girls, could not have guessed why he so fascinated his two most eager listeners. Judy says, "His hairless legs obsessed us. We used to gather in the common room and try to look peppy and alert. But whenever he crossed his legs, his pant leg would ride up and we could see these hairless legs. He was the one man we ever saw, and we were fixated on those legs. We managed to behave ourselves, but only if we didn't look at each other. We'd have to fight to keep ourselves from laughing."

But just as often as Judy laughed, she broke down in uncontrollable weeping. Karin was there to comfort her, but Judy could not relieve her terrible guilt. She couldn't understand why she was in the home. What had she done that was so wrong? Despite seeing the pastor as "a twit," she tried to seek help from the man with the hairless legs. "I was fairly religious up to that time," she says. "But when I went to Sterling I had done two years of university and I was questioning everything. I remember talking to him. I was feeling so bad, and he told me that Jesus forgave me. I wanted to say, 'For what? What are you talking about?' "

Judy didn't have the nerve to voice her silent question. Even to broach the subject would be heresy, a sure sign that she was not sorry for what she had done and the pain she had caused to others. The assumption that the girls had made a mistake, that it was all their fault, still makes Judy angry when she talks about her time at Sterling. "It was a beautiful home and kind of peaceful, but I didn't want to be there. I thought it was wrong that I should be there. We were treated condescendingly. It was like being in a nice prison. There was redemption somewhere for bad girls. But what we'd done was something shameful, very shameful."

Earlier, in the homes of the 1950s, religious instruction was rarely sugar-coated as talks or devotions. After she arrived in Canada, Janet Roberts had gone occasionally to services at the Baptist Church in Scarborough, where she had volunteered as a Guide and Brownie leader. Although it had been a church woman who had suggested the Bethel Pentecostal Home to her when she needed a place to go, Janet wasn't prepared for its fundamentalist atmosphere. "It was religion morning and night,"

Janet says. "It was similar to the Baptists, but a lot more vocal. We had to learn a lot of quotations from the Bible and we had homework. We got together every night and learned a new verse for the next night – things that would remind us of just who we were. It was like Sunday school, like kids in Sunday school, when they learn things for the next week. But it was our every-day activity. I guess it's an everyday activity for a normal Pentecostal family, too."

The two-generation family that ran the home had little to offer other than ardent religious practice. Making and enforcing rules and assigning chores seemed to be their only skills. The work the girls had to do was required not for purposes of social interaction but as a payment for food and shelter. For their privacy and their sins, the girls paid a price in elbow grease. There were a dozen or more girls as well as the two resident fam-ilies in the home, which meant the girls spent a lot of time in the kitchen and laundry. "We used to have to do a lot of work," Janet remembers. "A lot of work. We had to help with the cooking, with running the house, with everything. We were always doing canning and things like that, plus we had to keep the Harrisons' apartments clean. And because I had been trained as a children's nurse I also had to look after the two little kids."

Janet has mixed feelings about the work. She has no doubt that it was intended as a punishment. But she was also grateful to be kept busy. It helped her keep her mind off the baby she was carrying and her own future. In any case, there was nothing else to do. Walking in the back garden was allowed, but that was it. Shopping and visiting were not permitted. Janet had no one to visit with except her Aunt Vi, and didn't have any spending money anyway. Her aunt had to supply her with shampoo and deodorant. In other homes, sometimes a girl could get a bit of money for her work. If Pam G. had stayed on the garbage detail at the Our Lady of Mercy Home in Vancouver, she could have earned a few dollars a week. The Calgary Salvation Army paid three dollars a day to one girl who was willing to walk a mile each way to their seniors' residence and wash dishes. But usually the daily jobs were the girls' "contribution." Required, but expected to be given freely out of gratitude.

In other homes the labour the girls had to give was sometimes much heavier than the work Janet did at Bethel. The first maternity homes had helped pay their way by taking in laundry and were often better known to the public as commercial laundries. In the homes that were attached to hospitals this function continued well into the 1950s. Though the old washboards had long gone, there were still many hands that could be usefully deployed.

At the Salvation Army homes attached to the Grace hospitals, the girls' morning routine always started with a walk through the basement corridors that connected the houses with the hospitals. In the huge laundry rooms they would feed sheets through giant mangles. Others would work in twos, folding. The work was tiring and hot and sweaty. Sylvia J. was in the Army's Grace Haven Montreal home in the summer of 1952. Her strongest memory is of the sweltering heat in the laundry room and her discomfort as she bent down to take another load of hospital gowns and towels out of the industrial dryers. "I felt a bit resentful about doing that work," she says. "At home I never really had to do anything other than help with the dishes and make my bed. But here I felt like I was doing penance. They are a wonderful organization, but we were supposed to repent for our sins. There was no counselling like there would be today."

Sylvia's time in a laundry room that summer didn't end in the hospital basement. Back at the home in the evenings, the girls would have to wash their personal things. Or at least they pretended to. The room with the clunky old wringer machines was also where everyone escaped to smoke, until they were found out. It's a story that Sylvia takes some pleasure in telling: "The place was always blue with all of us puffing away, and one night the major came down and whipped the door open. She nearly choked to death on the smoke. We just cracked up."

The red face of the Army officer meant trouble, but it was funny to see and smoking was a minor sin to work off. Around the nuns and priests at the Misericordia Home in Edmonton, no one dared to break the rules. There, mass was compulsory at least once a day. If a girl momentarily forgot her shame, her punishment was swift and sometimes cruel. Loretta Fournier learned that lesson over and over again. In order to get to their meals in a separate building, the girls had to cross the hospital's inside courtyard. They were forbidden to laugh or play there, a ban that Loretta, who was just fourteen, had a hard time observing. A game of tag meant a visit to the priest for another lecture on her evil soul. "I was badly treated by the priests and the nuns – the dark people," she says. Once, she dared to go out for a walk with some of the older girls. "I was caned because I went to the riverbank. I have scars from that because I tried to run out. The priest said I was the devil's work, and I had to go on my knees and say that I was sorry. Sister Frances knew what went on, but she was a nun, and the priest was in charge. We had committed this mortal sin. I think she was really torn. She would never say that this is the wrong thing, but I knew from her eyes that she wished he wouldn't say that."

The compassionate Sister Frances doesn't see herself as the saint that Loretta makes her out to be, nor the others as the "dark" figures that frightened the fourteen-year-old. When I asked Sister Frances about Loretta's experience and that of others in the Catholic homes of the 1950s, she was circumspect. "Sometimes I would hear of it. I remember one experience, and I went to see the

Father right away. But the priest wasn't there for the girls, he was there for the hospital. So that was different. I don't remember the girls telling me any bad experiences and they were very open with me. It seems to me that if they'd had a bad experience they would have told me."

Perhaps Loretta's memories are exaggerated or perhaps she was too shy to report what really happened. Or perhaps Sister Frances is just being discreet. Certainly, I have heard stories about other nuns such as Sister Frances – nuns who had a loving manner, who saw their role as rescuer rather than judge. In describing to me how she saw her mission, Sister Frances chose one of the Bible stories that often appears in religious illustrations: Jesus rescuing the stray sheep. "He goes and gets that little sheep and leaves everybody else, and carries it in his arms and brings it back to the flock. To me, this is a beautiful image of what he does with the girls. I can't say that I preached a lot of this when the girls were with me, but I tried to love them as much as I could. And the Sisters that were with me were very, very kind to them also. We tried to show them all this kindness so they wouldn't feel all this shame."

Sister Frances knew that the Misericordia Home was not perfect – and she set out to create a better environment for the girls. By 1963, her prodigious efforts at fund-raising had secured a new building, away from the hospital grounds. Pineview had more space and more privacy. Here she could introduce many of the programs – including visits from various clergy – that she felt would help reduce the girls' sense of shame. But this came years too late for Loretta. In 1956, she felt Sister Frances' Christianity only as an occasional breeze that relieved the austerity of the Misericordia Home.

For a devout Catholic girl such as Loretta, the religious practice of the homes was a given. She accepted as her due the treatment she got from the "dark people" and sought solace in the warmth of Sister Frances. But the Misericordia was in fact open to all faiths. There were others who would not pay for their supper with an alien prayer.

Loretta's best friend at the home was a farm girl from Galahad, a minuscule town in southeastern Alberta. Aged eighteen, Sherry Bennett was a short, stocky blonde who hid the bruises of a background of sexual abuse under a tough, sometimes rebellious exterior. She had already left Galahad for agricultural college when she was called back home in the spring of 1956 to help her father with the planting. It was a blistering hot summer that year, and Sherry got so badly sunburned she had to wear a sugar sack, with eyeholes cut out, over her head so she could drive the tractor.

When she found out she was pregnant, Sherry decided to keep the child and raise it on her own. She knew she would be marked as a slut if she did so in Galahad, so she left again, without telling her parents anything. "I just disappeared," she says. "They sent out search parties. When I was out in B.C. I saw an article in the paper asking me to call home." But Sherry didn't want to hear what she figured she would. Anyway, she wasn't living on the streets; she'd got a job selling medical encyclopedias door to door, and thought she might make it on her own. "They would put a bunch of us in the car, and we would do these little towns. The company did not know that I was pregnant, and the other girls didn't immediately. When I got sick I said that I was car sick." But once Sherry's pregnancy began to show, she was fired. She tried a wage home in Vancouver that she says drove her "insane." Finally, faced with the reality of having to hide, she went back to Alberta, to Edmonton.

Sherry is a fighter, someone who always demands her rights. And at a time when an unmarried, pregnant girl was a social outcast, sticking up for herself took a good deal of courage. But she did even when she had to ask for help from the city's Social

Services. She is the only woman I've interviewed who asked any real questions about what options she had, grilling the flummoxed social worker about the differences among the three homes for unmarried, pregnant girls in Edmonton. Sherry didn't like the sound of the Beulah Home – "too much heavy religion." The small St. John's Home run by the Anglicans was full. If she had to be around any church, she thought she'd prefer the Roman Catholics, mostly because she'd seen priests with cigarettes and a glass of beer or two. "I thought the RC people did all these things that were forbidden. I related to that freedom better than the born-again Christian stuff." When she found out the girls could smoke at the Misericordia Home, she made up her mind. As soon as she got there, after mounting the rickety wooden steps up to the TV room on the second floor, she saw a group of pregnant girls lighting up. Just what she wanted. The Misericordia had met her number-one priority.

If there is one thing that unites the girls who ended up at homes for unwed mothers – apart from the obvious – it's their desire to smoke. Although in a few places girls had to sneak down to the laundry room, the turn-of-the-century rules stating "no tobacco . . . neither snuffing nor chewing" had largely disappeared. Smoking was not yet a health concern, and by the 1950s and 1960s most homes accommodated the girls' need to puff away. At the Misericordia in Edmonton, the nuns even encouraged the girls to smoke. Sherry says they were always telling the girls, "Sit down and have a smoke. It will help you relax."

Smoking wasn't bad, but there was still a long list of other transgressions an unwed mother could admit to and repent, particularly the one that had landed Sherry there. She was grateful to be able to smoke, but she wasn't going to go anywhere near the chapel she was encouraged to visit. Always resourceful, she found a way to avert the guilt she saw Loretta carry. "I was told that I could go to the chapel and pray. The nuns said it didn't matter to God what I was. But I decided that I didn't want to go to any damn chapel, so I chose my own church. My mother was Presbyterian. So I just trotted over there and got the whole sacrament. I did it almost right away. That's what saved me from the Roman Catholics. Of course I didn't go back to the Presbyterians either."

Sherry wasn't about to let anybody get away with anything she didn't like. She wasn't going to confess her sins, and she wasn't going to lose her individuality. All the girls there had to assume false names. For a long time, Sherry knew Loretta as "Rose." Only near the end did the younger girl trust Sherry enough to divulge her true, secret, identity. But Sherry argued to the nuns that as her real name was Sherone, she should be able to keep its short form. So she stayed Sherry. Of all the girls who were at the Misericordia with her, she alone remained herself – at least in name. But this was only one battle won and there was a long war to go.

A fight over the question of work assignments was out of the question. Although Sherry had managed to fudge on prayer, other duties were compulsory. Room and board, here as everywhere else, came with a price. There were no cooking chores, because the girls ate food prepared in the hospital. They did have to keep the dormitories clean, but sweeping and dusting wasn't considered a job. Their real work, the work they had to do, the work that was heartbreaking for most of the girls, was upstairs.

The third floor, above where the girls slept, was a nursery lined with dozens of baby cots. These were the children of the girls who had already left. The babies were kept in the nursery until they were adopted or sent off to an orphanage. In long day and night shifts, the new girls took care of the babies of the girls who had preceded them.

Sherry's description of what it was like – for the girls and the babies – is chilling. "They were kept there until they were two. If they weren't babies any more, they got shipped to another place. You knew if a child had Indian blood in him or her, they probably would not get a home. There was no choice about working up there. I could choose between working days with year-old babies, or nights with the little ones. I chose newborns. I worked all night with them. Nights went from 11 P.M. to 7 A.M. I would feed babies all night. There would be eight, maybe ten, babies in this nursery. Then I slept all day down in the dormitory, right next to the doorway where people came and went all day. There was no sound-proofing, and I could hear the washers and dryers clanking in the laundry downstairs and all the babies crying on the third floor. It was noisy, but I got used to it."

Working in the nursery, where they witnessed the fate of the babies they were carrying, was upsetting for most of the girls. Sometimes they would have to show off the babies to prospective adopting couples. Sister Frances shared their feelings. This wasn't the right kind of work for these girls. Though she is not outright critical, she does say, "I didn't appreciate that." Even as Sherry was working her night shifts in 1956, Sister Frances was trying to get the nursery moved, both to save the girls more pain and to find more space and privacy than the uncomfortable, overcrowded dormitories could supply. By the following year, the nursery was gone, and the third floor turned into a recreation area and single and double rooms for the girls. The girls who came after Sherry and Loretta weren't reminded every day of the babies they would not be able to keep.

At age fourteen, Loretta was considered too young to work with the babies. So she focused on her studies. Her father had always believed in education. He'd sent her away to a convent school when she was just eight partly for the opportunity to "better herself." Now she rediscovered his dream for her. She knew she couldn't throw herself down the stairs again, as she had done at the Good Shepherd, although she and the other girls used to talk about suicide all the time. Instead, she had a new goal: "I just knew if I got an education I would have a better life. That is what I held on to all the time." She took correspondence courses, which the nuns corrected. There was no schoolroom, so she spent most of the day sitting on her bed. After her lessons were finished, there were still hours to pass while the other girls worked upstairs in the nursery. "You just had to sit there. You thought about things, prayed and pondered, reflected upon your life. We were not encouraged to be friends with each other at all. That's why we had the phony names."

Through all those days she sat by herself in the dormitory while the girls from the night shift slept, Loretta clung to the one treasure she had brought with her. She still has it. It is a yellowed silk pillowcase sewn by her grandmother, an English woman who married a Métis. She never forgot her own roots. Across the silk she had embroidered "There'll always be an England." As her granddaughter waited out the days at the Misericordia, she clutched the pillow for security. The words became a mantra for Loretta. They reminded her that she was worth something. To her, they meant she had a respectable past and that she would have a future.

At the order's original home in Montreal, the girls also had a gruelling schedule. In the early days of La Miséricorde, the *filles-mères* had tended babies, too, before and even after their own child was delivered. In order to work off the cost of her room and board, each girl was required to stay at least six months after her baby was born, to wash and feed not only her own child but any others who were in the orphanage attached to the hospital. In 1932, as Andrée Lévesque found in the Misericordia archives, one girl wrote to her mother that she had been breast-feeding three or four babies. She had developed anemia and was being allowed to leave because she could no longer do her work. Another girl complained that she had been "doing 13 babies for 3 months, washing them, feeding them and scrubbing."

By 1964, when Marie Benoit arrived at La Miséricorde, the girls were no longer looking after babies – nurses now worked in the orphanage – but they still had to work for their food and shelter. While Protestant girls often went to a home to escape the bad treatment they had experienced in wage homes, at La Miséricorde the girls were sent out to do the same kind of work as domestics in private homes around Montreal. They were picked up by their employers in the morning and returned to La Miséricorde in the afternoon.

Marie had only just arrived at La Miséricorde and had not yet been given her outside work assignment when she witnessed a scene that convinced her she couldn't stay there. It was near suppertime on only her second or third day. She was sitting on her bed, worrying about what would happen next when, she says, "some of the girls started coming back from working out-side. We were getting ready for supper, when this one girl came in. It was springtime. I remember she had a light coat on. But she didn't take it off. She sat on the chair that was right near the door, and she started crying. Some of the girls went to see her, and everybody sort of joined around her after that. Because I was new, I didn't know anybody. She was sobbing, she was really sobbing. I could hear people saying, 'It's all right, it's okay. It will be all right.' I went over and asked what was happening. I was told this girl had just been raped by her employer. I started crying. I thought, What am I doing here? And they said, 'Look, this is happening all of the time, but we can't say anything because nobody believes us. They think we're no good anyway, so they just take advantage of us.' The girls couldn't tell the nuns what happened, because the girls would be accused of doing something that got them raped. I was so terrified. I came from a background of abuse, and I did not want to go through that again. One of the girls said to me, 'If you have money there is another place that you can go to.' I told her, 'I don't have any money.' She said, 'If you can pay later, there is a place that you can go. They don't advertise it, but you can pay after you come out.'"

Marie learned that the other place was also operated by Les Soeurs de la Miséricorde, and that it was indeed an option for girls who could afford it. When Marie asked the nuns if she could leave, they grilled her about why she wanted out and how she would pay for her keep. But Marie persisted, and a few weeks later she moved to the Villa St-Michel, on the boulevard of the same name, about a ten-minute drive away. Marie could tell, even from the outside, that money bought a much better environment. The villa was another huge home, with enough room for dozens of girls, but it was a warm-yellow brick building, set back from the busy street. There were trees and high hedges to hide the girls. In the back they could sit out on lawn swings. Inside, the girls were housed just two to a room, and each wing had a small kitchen, where the girls could make evening snacks. They had to keep their own area clean, including washing the floors, but this was a different world of work. You paid for the accommodation, but it was a straightforward money transaction.

The humiliation, however, continued. As Marie describes it, there was nothing different here about the way the girls were regarded by those in charge. "It would have been an ideal place for a girl to go and hide," she says, "except the nuns' attitude was the same as at the other place. They made you feel that you had to pay for your sins, and that you were very fortunate to be in a place like this. It was a 'We took you in' attitude, and 'You'd better do what we tell you. You're no good.' They would say to me, 'Well, what do you think would have happened to you if this place didn't exist?' Maybe I voiced my opinion a little bit too much. When something was unjust, some of the stuff going on with the girls, I would tell. And they said, 'You're here, who do you think you are?' Whatever you said, they would put you down. They never said a kind word."

In 1962, Linda Chalmers was also in the Catholic system, but at the brownstone on Stanley Street she'd gone to there were no nuns rustling up and down the stairs. In fact, there seemed to be no religious or moral agenda at all. Yet Linda was as frightened as Marie. "I hadn't been there very long when this terrible thing happened. In my room there was a girl from Nova Scotia, one from Montreal who was older, then another whose bed was right next to mine. She was definitely older than all of us, and I think she was mentally ill. She started to freak out in the middle of the night. She got out of bed and came over to where I was – I had a bed right next to the wall – and started to choke me. I was just terrified."

At fifteen Linda wasn't as worldly as the twenty-year-old Marie, who had been out working for several years. She didn't know where else she could go. After begging her mother just a week earlier to get her out of the wage home she hated so much, Linda was afraid to tax her mother's patience by demanding to be moved again. She did ask to move beds, but then she withdrew. She did her chores – the evening dishes and polishing the brass banister in the front hall – but she was careful to keep to herself. Other contact was either dangerous or forbidden. "I didn't talk to the other girls much, especially after that girl attacked me," she says. "If I had to tell you one conversation, I couldn't. Nobody made close friends there. It was very much drilled into your head that no close contact was allowed. Anyway, if you did get to know somebody, she would just be going off soon and you'd never see her again. And, of course, you wouldn't know her real name, anyway."

Beth Holmes was used to domestic work. It's all she'd ever done since she'd quit school at age sixteen. So she knew all about cleaning and laundry and peeling vegetables. But when I asked if she had to do anything like that at Molly Breen's, she said she couldn't remember doing any chores. "We were responsible for our own side of the beds, our own piece of the room that we had, but I don't remember doing a dish or sweeping a floor," she says. "There was a young woman who did help, Cecilia. I think Molly introduced her to some buddy down the street and they got married. It could very well be that we had to work, but I don't think so."

When I asked Molly Breen about whether the girls helped out, she couldn't believe I was serious. "Oh, no, ducky, I didn't think I should make them work. They had enough trouble." So Molly paid Cecilia (whom she did fix up with "a nice young man, and they're still together") to do the housework, while she reigned in the kitchen, a one-woman dynamo turning out jelly rolls and turkey pies.

As for religion, the various churches may have had a piece of most institutions in Newfoundland, but not Molly's. "I've never seen the inside of a church since I was married," Molly says. She associated the churches with judgement, and she didn't believe in blaming "these poor little things." They weren't sinners to her, just human beings.

But Molly herself was judged by plenty of good, upstanding Christians for taking in "girls like that." Even her own sister turned up her nose at what Molly was doing. "I was condemned for having them," she says. "My sister said to me one day, 'Molly, what have you got them cattle in here for?' Yes, that's what she said." When Molly told me this I was stunned for a minute. Cattle? Then I asked what she'd said to her sister. "I think I slapped her. And I told her, 'Don't ever say anything like that again.' She was vexed with me for a long time."

Molly Breen's no-religion, no-work rules were the exception in those days. In homes all across Canada girls prayed and worked to earn their keep, and many of us appreciated the order and conformity of the homes. By toeing the line here, regardless of whether the work was light or onerous, the sermons slight or shaming, a girl could feel that she was regaining some of the status and normalcy she had so obviously lost. As one woman who stayed in a Protestant home in Montreal says, "I guess we were really good girls, because nobody caused any problems when I was there. We all acted like ladies. Nobody really cursed or swore. I'm not saying somebody didn't say 'shit' once in a while, but mostly we behaved like ladies." Another girl in a Catholic home felt blessed to be there. "It was a sanctuary for me. I don't remember there being very many rules, but maybe that was because I was in no position to be going out and doing anything the nuns wouldn't have approved of."

"I was in no position." That's a phrase we all would have used then. Sociologist Prudence Mors Rains points out in her American study that "because the girls felt a particular vulnerability to questions of good taste and respectability, they were inclined when left to the dictates of conscience to make the most morally conservative decision." We knew we had done something very wrong. This was the only place that would take us in. If we could be good here, if we said our prayers and did our chores, we would not only get out, we might even be forgiven. We could start again. If we learned how to follow the rules, surely we wouldn't get in trouble again.

# 4

# *Boyfriends, Lovers, and Other Strangers*

*"Nowhere does the biological difference between man and woman
stand out in its social implication so much as in the difference
between an unmarried mother and an unmarried father. The
biological burden is entirely upon the unmarried mother, as it
is on all mothers, but in the great majority of instances the
unmarried father escapes any responsibility."*
– N. Reider, *American Journal of Orthopsychiatry,* 1948

As I washed my floors and lined up for meals, and the days and
weeks went by, it became harder and harder for me to remember
that I'd led a much different life just a few months earlier. Even
the story I kept telling myself about what had happened began to
sound false, or at least hollow. I had been in love, I thought – and
I had been loved, I thought, so why was I here? I must have done
something very wrong.

In the manner of the guilty, I marshalled my defence. At least
I had waited before I'd made my mistake. For a teenager in the
late 1950s and early 1960s, sex was like fashion. There was a set
of rules that you knew by heart and broke at your peril. Never
wear blue with green; touching allowed over, but not under,
your clothes. No white after Labour Day; petting above the

waist but not below. It was always so far and no further, with alarm bells drowning out any notes of physical pleasure. My only official sex education was a few tense minutes with my mother that took place for some reason in our kitchen broom closet. It came to a merciful end when she gave up trying to explain anything and handed me the pamphlet that the Kotex company used to publish, *You're A Young Woman Now*. Other details I learned from girlfriends, who usually had it wrong themselves. But we all knew enough to know what getting pregnant would mean. And it was terror of pregnancy, not any moral rectitude, that had kept me pure until I went to Vancouver.

Fear was helped in my case by the awkwardness of most of the boys I knew. None of them could match my early fantasies of a Pat Boone, "Love Letters in the Sand" kind of romance. As my cultural horizons broadened, they didn't have a chance. Ayn Rand may not have written great literature, but when I somehow got my teenage hands on *The Fountainhead*, I was hooked on Howard Roark. It was not romance, but passion I lusted after. In my daydreams I was Dominique Francon, a strong woman but still vulnerable to a heroic yet haunted man. Melodramatic, yes, but I suspect this was the fantasy nursed by many young women in those years.

I thought I had found what I wanted when I moved to Vancouver. He was older, he was a poet and a painter, he was poor and rebellious, and he wanted me. Of course it sounds silly now, as intense young love always does to those who look back in reason. But I believed then – and I still want to – that my feelings were true. Most important, I believed they were reciprocated.

Of course I worried about pregnancy. But even in the late 1960s, an unmarried girl could not just ask for the birth-control pill. When I did find the nerve to go to a doctor, I carefully picked a woman physician's name from the phone book. But her sex gave me no protection. After I blurted out my request, she shook her head in sadness and disapproval, then took me into a tiny room and showed me a film strip about venereal disease. Between risking that kind of shame again in a quest for the pill and trusting my lover, it was not hard to choose.

I had judged badly. Of course I should have known, but I had no reason – or perhaps desire – to doubt his story about the unhappy marriage he had left behind in another city. Of course I – we – would be different. I imagined us living some perfect bohemian life in a garret apartment, drinking red wine from raffia-wrapped bottles, munching on crusty French loaves, and bringing home bunches of fresh flowers every day.

Like so many girls who found themselves alone and pregnant, I didn't want to hear the blame that, in those days, would have come from every corner. Or the sympathy for a sweet young thing betrayed by a cad. So I didn't talk about what had happened. I had told my best friend, Sonja, but no one else. How could I convince my middle-aged, middle-class parents that I had been in love? Would a social worker think better of me for that? Even at Maywood, who among these silly girls would understand my story? And what would thin-lipped, abstemious missionaries know about passion?

But talking to the other girls now, as grown women, I realize how similar we were. No one wanted to talk about why she was at the home. We all knew the sin we had in common. It was sex. We had "done it." Because we had no wedding rings, we couldn't call it "making love." But semantics hardly mattered; no one talked about "it" anyway. Neither the girls nor the staff. Once in the home, normal teenage talk about sex ceased almost completely. Racked with guilt, we recoiled from the subject that was our downfall. The staff was content to consign the act to the past, because their orientation was the future.

They hoped to ensure we would never do "it" again, not without benefit of clergy.

Almost all the homes claimed to be non-judgemental. In old Salvation Army pamphlets describing the Bethany and the Grace Haven homes, it is the "loving and supportive atmosphere" that is always mentioned. The Sisters of the Misericordia declared that only the "compassion of the heart to the most abandoned" guided their work. Humewood House in Toronto described itself as "a place of understanding," adding, "Those who work here are here to help and never to judge." But how free from judgement could they be? Where had these moral dicta come from but the church – any church, all the churches. They were hiding girls they had helped to condemn. They were not out on the streets trying to change societal attitudes. Regardless of what they may have said or written about their mission, by the very service they provided they were acknowledging and accepting the public scorn that stigmatized us all.

There was no talk of the fathers, either. In 1964, when the representatives from homes for unmarried mothers gathered for the Out of Wedlock conference in Toronto, the fathers were hardly mentioned. There is only one reference in the published proceedings to the other half of "the causes of illegitimacy and extra-marital pregnancy." One speaker asked, "Who is the man or boy who impregnated the girl? What is he like? What of his home background? Is he passive and dependent or aggressive and sexually overwhelming? Is he as irresponsible in other areas of his behaviour as well? Does he have an ego deficiency that shows up in his inability to care for or relate to a woman?" These are interesting questions. But when the speaker suggested to her audience, "Perhaps some of you have opinions along these lines that we could share," there was no response. The issue of the father was not brought up again. Instead, the discussion went on to morals, values, the dangers of "steady dating among teenage girls." The focus was on the girls, even though it took two to tango.

As you would expect, there were no "impregnated girls" at this conference. They might have had some interesting observations to make about the other half of their dilemma. But neither at the conference nor in the homes did the father have much presence. In the social-work jargon of the day he was the "putative father," or just the PF. He came into the picture if money was an issue or to complete the adoption procedure. Even then, only his medical history and physical features were of interest. When workers in the homes tried to show some sensitivity about the issue of the fathers, all too often they just invoked the old stereotype of the victimized girl. As one Salvation Army officer in a Calgary home put it, "I would blame the guys. I don't think the girls would ask for sex, would they? In my mind I always felt that they were taken advantage of."

Ironically, for me, it was a man – another man – who helped me through my time at the home. My "putative father" had disappeared. Occasionally I would get a romantic letter, but that gesture didn't have much power over me any more. I knew I was on my own. After my mother had gone and the plan to go to the home was settled, I had a couple of months to wait, so I continued at school, hiding inside my big black cape. Once, after a class in Romantic poetry, as the professor was returning essays, he complimented me on my work. This prompted another student, a young, naïve-looking boy, to suggest we go for coffee. We both loved literature, and the time passed easily as we compared notes on Wordsworth and Coleridge, then moved on to T. S. Eliot and Ezra Pound, ee cummings and Wallace Stevens. After weeks of skulking around, I was having my first real conversation with anyone. It felt wonderful, but at the same time

I felt nervous about having a secret I couldn't share. I decided it was best to stay away from any new friendships. Eventually I scurried away with some manufactured excuse, planning to avoid him in the future.

Not long afterwards, he appeared at my door one rainy evening. Looking like a shiny little kid just out of the bath, he simply said, "I think you're in some kind of trouble, and I want to help." Such an open and guileless invitation washed my resolve away, and I told him everything. Perhaps my situation just seemed poetic to him, but he became my best friend. We spent most of our time together. From him I got comfort, support, and laughter. He couldn't understand why I was going into a home – the "lock-up," as he called it. "Why don't you just stay with me?" he asked repeatedly. I told him he didn't understand the rules. I had to hide, if not for me then for the other people I had hurt and embarrassed. I loved his daring, but it wasn't mine any more.

When I went into the home, he remained my lifeline. At the end of term he had to return home to Calgary, but until then he brought a touch of chivalric warmth to my isolation. I would get passes out of the home to meet him. In between visits he wrote to me constantly, and I wrote back. I think now he imagined me to be some princess locked in a tower. If he couldn't save me, at least he could be faithful. Best of all, he didn't judge me.

Perhaps he was one of the reasons I didn't make friends at the home. Before I got pregnant I had always had close female friends. At Maywood, after my initial dismissal of the other girls, I did try to get to know them. For the first week or so I would go down to the smoking room. As the officers didn't smoke, I thought that the talk would be freer there. But the girls seemed to have little in common with me as they talked about hairdos and clothes and what guy had a neat car. Of course, no one was supposed to talk about the past, that was another of the rules. So we couldn't talk about what we did have in common. But, to tell the truth, I didn't give anyone a chance.

Writing a book like this one with any honesty means you have to face up to your past, not only what was done to you, but what you might have done to others. I have often asked myself why I didn't make more of an effort to connect with those other girls. At school I had overcome a natural shyness and had always taken leadership roles. I was often at the centre of some new activity. I knew what effort that usually took, and at the home I had no energy for performance and, more important, no desire for recognition. Although I had always sought approval, now I did not want it. Another self emerged at Maywood – an odd mixture of old and new. In many ways, I retreated to being a quiet, insecure, thin-skinned girl who felt any criticism as a mortal blow. I projected my own shame onto the other girls and then kept my distance. At the same time, that distance marked what little pride I had left. I was not going to give up my new sense of adulthood completely. I did not like the consequences of my actions any more than anyone else, but I was still some- where, in some confused way, proud that I had acted.

Still, I regret that I didn't, or couldn't or wouldn't, get my mind off my own troubles long enough to find out about what had happened to those other girls and young women, to learn why they were there, to hear about what man or boy had been a part of their lives for however long, however briefly. In many ways, this chapter is an attempt to make up for that. Although my old coldness to them was perhaps a necessary defence at the time, and although they probably didn't give me a second thought except to dismiss me as stand-offish or snobbish, the way I treated them was exactly the same way that too many others did – I was just like the society and the system that did not want to hear or believe their stories. I blamed, I dismissed, I did not want to see myself in them. But each of these girls had a tale of love or betrayal, or something far worse. I like to think the stories that follow are at least a start to the listening I didn't do thirty years ago.

When she was at Sterling in Oakville, Karin was lucky to have her friendship with Judy. Like me, they found the other girls at the home very young and dismissed them in the teen talk of the day as "be-boppers." The two of them stuck together, forming a kind of defensive front, sharing what had happened to them only with each other.

Karin could handle herself, she thought. She hadn't wanted to marry Bill, the father of the baby, so she wasn't going to moan about any lost loves. Besides, she felt she had no right to moan. She was no abandoned, naïve girl. It was she who had broken up with Bill. They had been going together for about a year. Although she was fond of him and found him quite sensitive, she couldn't see any future for them as a couple. So one snowy winter night she arranged to meet Bill in a park to tell him it was all over. "Finished, no more," she says. Had the relationship ended there, she might not have found herself six months later at a home for unwed mothers. But she had one dramatic flourish left. "A couple of days later I went back to get my stuff and made love with Bill. It was a final goodbye, and it was very romantic. Somehow having sex with him at that point seemed important. It was a farewell. It was sentimental, but it also got me knocked up."

Karin was not quite the sweet young thing, seduced and abandoned by a predatory male. But neither was she a party girl who asked for sex. She is not shy about admitting that she had "done it" more than once with Bill. She sees herself as a typical teenager of her time. "It was 1964," she says. "The whole attitude was changing. I think that is important to remember. The pill was just beginning to come in. We read about it in the newspapers. You could only get it if you were married. But you'd had pressure on you since you were sixteen, and now you're almost twenty, and there's curiosity and hormones and other things. There was an immense amount of pressure. And not just from boys; it was everywhere."

Virginity – and when to "lose" it – was a huge issue for teenage girls in the early 1960s. The old rule (never before marriage) was breaking down, but the sexual revolution was still waiting in the wings. Most parents – that is, most mothers – like mine, were usually too embarrassed to talk to their children about sex. There was no sex education in the schools. A girl was left on her own to make her way through the moral minefield of the day.

Often it seemed that you couldn't win, no matter what you did. Doug Owram, a history professor at the University of Alberta, describes the sexual politics of the time in his book *History of the Baby-Boom Generation*: "As children, baby-boomers received contradictory messages. The 1950s and early 1960s were more liberal than previous decades, but the changes were partial rather than complete, limited to rhetoric and depiction rather than action, oriented more towards men than towards women. Most of all, old and new values sat uneasily juxtaposed. Everywhere the children coming into adolescence were more exposed to sexual display than their parents or grandparents had been. Yet the belief remained that sexual purity (redefined in slightly less onerous terms) was essential, especially for girls."

Dating was the game, but how did you play it? If you went "all the way," you were a tramp. If you went so far and no more, you were a tease or "frigid" – almost as bad as being a tramp. These labels were out there, and they were used, and they hurt. At seventeen, virginity had become a burden Karin wanted to get rid of. She and a girlfriend set out to do just that. They checked into a cheap motel with their current boyfriends, determined to get it over with. After a few beers, her girlfriend did, but Karin passed out. "The next morning we all got up and went to breakfast. Jane wasn't a virgin any more, but I still was."

At Sterling, Karin's open talk about sex was all new to Judy. She thought about "it," but had assumed she was the only one who did. She remembers vividly how shocked she was one day at high school in the locker room after a volleyball game, when one of the girls started talking about her new boyfriend. "It's never going to happen to me," the girl said confidently. That was the first time Judy realized that other girls considered "it." Years later she met someone from her old school who'd had to get married. She laughed at Judy's naïveté. "Didn't you know that everyone was doing it?" Judy didn't.

In her second year at university, Judy met Tom and went to bed with him in a stew of emotions. "I was always terrified of getting pregnant and I never wanted to do it, but when I was going with Tom, it was kind of like an urge or something. Something you wanted to do. I think that it was physical as well as emotional." When a psychiatrist much later asked if she'd ever had an orgasm, she says, "I remember thinking, What's that? I don't think I knew exactly what an orgasm was, but there was a hormonal thing, or a desire to have sex. Nothing like, This is – wow! It was more a need to be loved."

Very few girls could enjoy sex much even if they did freely choose it. It was dangerous territory, which might be thrilling, but also too unsettling to be genuinely pleasurable. Although women's magazines, such as *Chatelaine*, were beginning to broach touchy subjects in articles such as "Is There a New Teenage Morality?" these were tentative explorations, usually ending with homilies such as this from the May 1963 issue: "They need more responsibilities to give them a challenge in life that will deflect them from turning to sexual experimentation for adventure." Only the most sophisticated young woman in those days would have had a liberated view of her own sexuality. Open discussion of female sexuality lay years ahead. Even though Judy at twenty was surely mature enough to feel genuine physical desire, she was still shadowed by the overwhelming social condemnation of premarital sex. For their part, the boys may have seemed to be confident, ready to pounce whenever they could, but that was often a pose. Several decades later, Judy takes a sympathetic view of Tom. "I think he was as nervous as I was, to tell you the truth. I can remember the first time that we did it, he kept saying that that was really bad and that we could never do that again. He was going on and on about how we are responsible to God, and everything else. Much later, he told me that that was the first time for him, too. I actually believe that was true."

Why didn't they use birth control then, especially if they were both afraid? Even if the pill was difficult for an unmarried girl to get, what about condoms? What about condoms, indeed. Perhaps it is hard to believe now at a time when condoms are available from dispensers in high-school washrooms, but until 1969 the dissemination of contraception – or even information about contraception – was illegal. A Toronto pharmacist was jailed in 1960 for selling condoms. Condom was the medical term; the street name was sheath or rubber, ugly words to connote unpleasant practices. They were for sale, but only behind the counter. How could you find the words for what you wanted? Judy and Tom used to sit in the car in front of drug-stores, arguing about who should go in for them. Tom said it would be easier for her because she was a girl. Judy tried, but she couldn't face the druggist in the white coat, who she was sure would look like her father. When she did find some condoms in her father's drawer, his wrath was an even more terrifying prospect. "I remember seeing them and thinking, I know what they are," she says. "I really lusted after them and wanted to steal one, but I was terrified. Can you imagine, if he knew that his daughter was taking his condoms? It would be worse than stealing money. I figured if they ever thought that I did anything, my life was over."

When, inevitably, Judy got into "trouble," she found she didn't have Tom to depend on, or anyone else. Tom, too afraid to buy condoms, promised to find an abortionist. But Judy had waited too long – she couldn't face the truth until it was unavoidable. By now it was five months, too late. Judy's parents wanted them to get married. Judy agreed and arranged everything, even finding an Anglican church in downtown Kingston so their neighbours wouldn't know. The ceremony would be small, and just family. But this shotgun wedding blew up in the bride's face.

"The day we were supposed to get married, I remember waking up and not feeling like you are supposed to feel on your wedding day. I woke up thinking, Oh, man, I've *got* to get married. It was terrible. It was scary, really scary. I didn't want to get married. But I was going to have a child. I couldn't just take off. Then at ten o'clock the minister called me and said he wasn't 'a marrying Sam.' We hadn't gone through a course, he said, and now he'd had second thoughts and decided he wasn't going to marry us. My mother got hysterical, saying we had to go to a Justice of the Peace, and then Tom called up and said, 'Well, the minister is probably right.' And I'm like, 'Okay.' And after that I was sent off to Sterling."

In the home, if the girl was still seeing the father, she might be able to add him to her list of allowed visitors. Though some places frowned on contact with the PF, others encouraged it. Except for conversion, there was no greater joy for home staff than the announcement of a marriage. Sometimes the vows were exchanged in the home. Marian W. remembers how all the girls in her home were required to attend one resident's wedding, complete with gifts and a bouquet to be caught. But, for Marian, the forced celebration only emphasized her own hopeless situation.

Judy didn't get another chance at a white dress. Tom kept in touch in a desultory way. Once, he came to visit. He said they should get married when it was "right." Judy should have a proper wedding, in a white dress, with all their friends and relatives there. But that would be after she got out. He didn't even mention the child. So much had happened so fast, Judy couldn't sort out her feelings. "Was I still in love with him?" she asks. "When you look back, can you call that love? But I was hurt – deeply hurt. I don't think I got over it for years and years. It was one of those things that haunted me, the fact that he didn't stay with me, and that it was such a shameful thing. I didn't believe it was shameful, but everybody else did, or appeared to."

Everyone except Karin. Karin was Judy's rock. But even though Karin seemed to be handling everything matter-of-factly, she had her own mortification to face. She hadn't asked Bill for anything so she didn't expect his betrayal. It came when the home required information about the father for adoption purposes. Karin readily gave his name, but when he was contacted, Bill denied he was the father. Karin was humiliated, but she wasn't going to be crushed. If she was so bad, at least she would laugh about it.

She got over her dashed romance by splurging on love comics. When they were feeling blue, Karin and Judy would lie on one of their beds, "huge as houses," and read smuggled comics aloud, with their own knowledgeable additions. "Oh, Sue," Judy would simper the words in the balloon above the lantern-jawed

hero, "I'll wait for you forever." "Until," Karin would impro-
vise, "the next blonde comes along." They thought they were
hilarious. And they felt better.

It's hard to imagine Janet Roberts and the other girls at the
Bethel Home on Kennedy Road in Scarborough giggling over
love comics. A Pentecostal shelter – with "religion day and
night" – didn't tolerate any talk about boys or sex. This was
almost a decade earlier. In 1957, nice girls weren't supposed to
think about sex, let alone joke about it.

Janet hadn't heard anything from Rolf, the putative father,
after she refused to have an abortion. But, like Bill, he was
tracked down. Then, as now, help for unwed mothers was not a
popular tax expenditure. For the small subsidies governments
gave to the homes, every province required the father to be
named, so he could be tracked down and made to pay. The legal
process was often pushed to the limit, although just as often as
not it backfired. As late as 1969, one Edmonton girl stood trembling outside a law court as a social worker prepared her to
testify about the paternity of her baby. In the courtroom the
young man, like so many before and after him, simply swore his
denial. It was her word against his. In a 1957 report, the
Canadian Welfare Council noted, "Failure of agencies to gain
[the putative father's] general co-operation is probably due in
part to the emphasis that has been placed on securing financial
assistance from him."

Janet was spared that courtroom drama, but she never knew
if Rolf took any responsibility. She didn't pay anything to the
home, so it's possible that he did. He certainly had enough
money. She heard that the home had been in contact with him,
both for money and background information, but she never
learned his response. Later she found out that he came to the

house on Kennedy Road once, to the front office where the girls were not allowed. Janet wasn't told he was there. And he didn't ask to see her.

The closest anyone at Bethel came to talking about men or sex was the Bible. The verses the girls had to learn every night were unequivocal about the sin they had committed. Both the New and the Old Testaments spoke directly about their sinfulness: "Watch and pray, that ye enter not into temptation: the spirit indeed is willing, but the flesh is weak," and "Homes are made by the wisdom of women, but are destroyed by foolishness." The son of the couple who ran the home usually led the evening devotion. He was a Pentecostal pastor, who also lived in the house with his wife. Janet says there was some distance between what he preached and what he practised.

"My job was to clean the top floor, and that's where he and his wife and two children lived, up on the top floor. That was one of my jobs, to help out with the children a bit and clean up the top, because they liked me, being fresh from England. But he'd always find excuses to come up there and flirt, and that was pretty scary. It was more than flirting. He didn't ever touch me because I said I would scream at the top of my voice if he ever touched me. He just kept coming closer and saying, 'We're alone now.' And I was so young and so naïve. I'd love to see him now. I'd let him know I remembered."

The pastor's wife was "really sweet, really nice," Janet says. "I don't know how she put up with him. I think she did know what he was doing because she'd always come upstairs and say, 'How are you coming along?' I'd say, 'I'm getting along fine, I'm nearly finished.' I think she came up to see where her husband was. I'm pretty sure. But she was so nice that you didn't want to hurt her. She had two nice children, too."

As the homes were largely communities of women, sexual threats from men of the cloth were more the exception than the rule. But the theological fears implanted by priests and ministers were often just as frightening, particularly for devout Catholic girls such as Loretta Fournier. As Mary G. Durkin says in her book *Feast of Love*, young girls growing up as Catholics in the 1950s were taught that "the only non-sinful kiss was one that caused feelings similar to what we would experience if we were to kiss a lamppost. Necking and petting were obviously evils to be avoided . . . Any action that resulted in the arousal of passion was evil and, therefore, must be avoided." Obviously, the girls who came to the Misericordia Home had gone beyond lamppost embraces. Here, too, there would be no sympathetic talk about love or sex, especially not with such an obvious sinner as Loretta, whose mortal errors included being both Métis and raped.

Night after night Loretta would wake up terrified by the images that haunted her dreams – the bedroom door being forced open, the bedclothes being ripped back. Her father knew she had been raped, but when he tried to have Jack charged the case fell apart. The court's blame fell on Loretta instead. As so often happens, the victimized girl became the criminal. Michael Sedlack, an American historian of adolescent deviancy, describes the double standard of those days: "Misbehavior on the part of boys is seen as non-sexual, normative, a phase which virtually all males go through and eventually grow out of and which will have few permanent serious consequences, either to the child or to society. In contrast, female delinquency, because of its sexual nature, is treated as behaviour that is dangerous, potentially contaminating, with long-term consequences."

Loretta did not understand what she had done wrong, but, she reasoned, she must have been very bad if she had to be locked up. It's probable that others sentenced to the Good Shepherd reform school were as confused as she was. Like other, similar institutions of the day, this facility for children did not distinguish between children who had committed crimes and those who had been abused or neglected. They were all housed together and treated alike. When Loretta was transferred to the Misericordia Home, the assumptions about her behaviour continued. As the priest told her that first day, she was "the devil's work."

In the same way that Karin and Judy gave each other support, Loretta found solace in her friendship with Sherry. But these two didn't talk about teenage dating and middle-class romances. Both their lives had been studies in misery from almost the beginning. Although Sherry was older by four years, their common experiences with sex had left them both angry and guilty. Both had uncles who had used the protection of the family to take advantage of them. Loretta's Uncle Jim used to try to fondle her, often in front of her mother, who did nothing to stop her brother. Sherry's Uncle Don forced himself on her from when she was just three until she was eleven years old. When she finally "told" on him, her mother refused to believe her. When Sherry was thirteen she was raped by one of the good citizens of Galahad. This time she told a neighbour, but she met the same rejection. "After I was raped I was crying all by myself, and Mrs. James, a lady from the community, took me aside and asked me what I was crying about, and I told her. I confessed the whole thing to her. And she said, 'How could you do that to your mother who is pregnant?' She just laid this whole guilt trip on me about how it was all my fault. And that I had it coming. So I learned very quickly not to confess."

But she could tell Loretta. Whenever they had any free time the two girls used to escape the home and walk along the river-bank that was just a block away from the hospital. Even in a cold Edmonton December they would go there to smoke cigarettes and talk about the past and the future. They wondered about what they had done wrong, how much of it had been their fault.

If everyone said it was their fault, surely it must have been. They often talked about suicide. But they were still young enough to have dreams about the future. They buried the bad memories under the fantasies they used to get them through.

Sherry's dream was marriage. She was convinced the father of her baby would come around. Ken was a country boy who had shown up one day the previous summer, out of the clear blue prairie sky, knocked on the door, and asked her out to a drive-in movie. "Ken was good-looking," Sherry says. "He was my size. I liked guys who were my size; at least then I could fight them off, somehow. He had the most beautiful eyes you ever saw, blue and big. That is, behind his Coke-bottle glasses. And he spoke ve-r-y, ve-r-y sl-o-o-w-ly. But he loved to dance. He took me to dances all the time and to the movies. His sister had a brain tumour. They took her to the States to have it removed, and it grew back. Ken and I used to take her to the drive-in with us. Then he would take her back up the hill home. Then we would have our sexual relationship."

Birth control was not an issue for Sherry. Nor was sex, for that matter. It was what you did if somebody asked, or demanded. That's what she'd learned from Uncle Don. The pattern was set. Sex was how you earned love. And she wanted love and babies. Sherry thought her relationship with Ken would lead to marriage. But he didn't have the same domestic view of the future. "He told me he marked down every time we had sex. He literally told me how many times we'd had sex when I told him I was pregnant. He didn't sweep me into his arms like I expected. He just said in his slow way, 'I gu-e-ss I'll ha-ve to th-i-ink a-bout it.' So while he was thinking, I said, 'Fuck you, man!' and I was gone out of there. I just ran to the city, because if I'd stayed there I would just be the slut my family always said I was."

Still, Sherry couldn't give up the idea of marriage. It was what she wanted and it would solve everything. Ken sent her money and came to visit her a couple of times at the home. They would sit in the car and talk. He never made any promises, but Sherry was sure one day they'd live "happily ever after." Loretta believed her older friend's dream. "I thought that it would all work out for her," she says. "Because that is what kept her together through all of this, the idea that he would come back and they would ride off into the sunset, with the baby. She was devastated when he didn't. But Sherry still hung on because she thought that the baby would make a difference and it would all work out. We all needed to hang on to something."

Loretta, too, found something to hang on to. There was the dream of education, the learning that would get her through. But she also worked hard at trying to be like Sherry and the other girls who talked about men and marriage. Sherry's confidence about Ken helped Loretta find a fantasy of her own. She fixated on a boy from her home town she liked and dreamed of a future with Johnny Rogers. She imagined he was crazy about her. She planned a wedding and thought about how she would fix up their house. She planned for the babies they would have. She was only trying to keep up, but it helped.

By her insistence on getting out of the order's downtown home in Montreal, Marie Benoit escaped the prisonlike atmosphere that Sherry and Loretta found at the Edmonton Misericordia. But, although the order's St-Michel home in Montreal had craft rooms and kitchenettes, she still found herself in an environment of judgement. "It would have been an ideal place to hide," she says, "except the nuns' attitude was not any different than at the other place." There was probably a good reason. By 1960, the first waves of Vatican II may have been lapping on the shores of the Roman Catholic maternity homes, but there was no forgiveness for Marie. She had a double shame to bear. She had a record. Marie was a recidivist. This was her second child to be born out of wedlock.

When I started searching for women who had been in homes for unwed mothers, I doubted the warnings that I would meet women who had been through the system twice. I couldn't believe that anyone would let it happen again. But I soon learned this was not uncommon. Marie's story is not unique. A woman from Brandon, Manitoba, had a first baby when she was fifteen at the Salvation Army home in Winnipeg, then another when she was eighteen, this time going into a Catholic home. A Montreal woman told me she was in a home in 1959, then four years later became pregnant again. Unwilling to go back to a maternity home, she managed on her own the second time, hiding in a cheap tenement. Another remembers the older woman who sat rocking by herself in a Regina home. She was rumoured to have had four or five illegitimate children. Others recall roommates who were a bit "retarded" and pregnant with their second or third child.

Obviously, some of these repeaters were deeply disturbed, or mentally challenged. They needed specialized help and didn't belong in a home. Those tragic stories I could understand. But the others? Normal, healthy women proving to be two- or three-time losers? Initially, I found it difficult to have any sympathy for them. I think some of that response was my ego talking: I had done my penance and had learned my lesson, why hadn't they? But, then, what was the lesson to learn except for abstinence? As I listened to their stories, the repeaters came to seem more inevitable than odd.

In many cases they came from horrific family situations – usually because of alcohol or sexual abuse or both – and they had returned to them. Finding no security there, their sad and unsuccessful search for acceptance and love continued, unchanged. They often fell into relationships with the kind of men who knew intuitively how to take advantage of vulnerable girls. Or perhaps the girls sought out men with whom they could have the only kind of relationship they knew. Only luck could save them from a second pregnancy.

The homes themselves contributed to a girl's second visit. After her first stay in a home, no one left with any knowledge about how to prevent a second pregnancy. The churches and religious sponsors would not do anything that could be seen as promoting premarital sex. That would violate their principles. They would not even consider preparing a girl for an activity that they did not condone. When I asked Captain Jolly what birth-control information she had dispersed in the 1960s, she replied, "Well, I told them they might face temptation again when they left and I advised them to talk to their family doctors." From her Army perspective, that was a liberal answer, but perhaps not so useful for the girls. By calling sex a "temptation" she was declaring it a sin. And few girls would have the courage to ask the avuncular doctor who had watched them grow up for assistance in being bad. For Catholic girls, contraception was a matter of dogma, and for the Church and the Sisters who ran the homes, that dogma was an inviolable principle. Sister Frances Cabrini told me she taught sex education at Pineview, but a resident from 1965 remembers only being shown the same kind of film strip about venereal disease that I was enlightened by. The dictum from the priests that they should keep their legs crossed wasn't of any more help to traumatized and troubled young girls. No one left one of these homes intending to return, but many were doomed to come back.

The first time Marie got pregnant was in 1959 when she was just fifteen, a lost child from a broken home, taking whatever affection she could find. Having heard the rumours about how girls were treated at La Miséricorde, an aunt had hidden her for the nine months and they had left the baby at the Miséricorde orphanage. Five years later, Marie was pregnant again. "The first time was very stupid," she says. "I didn't even know. I was just so stupid. This guy really did take advantage of me. I found out that he took advantage of a lot of girls, too. The second time it was a different thing. I was really in love with that man. And contraceptives weren't something that I ever considered. I would even say that I didn't mind getting pregnant. I didn't plan it, but I didn't do anything to stop it. Not that I wanted to get pregnant, but maybe what I was trying to do was replace my child that I had lost. Subconsciously, you know."

Nowadays, we might treat such issues of intention with compassion. But in 1964 no one tried to look for any subconscious reasons to explain why Marie was going through the system a second time. When the nuns at Villa St-Michel treated her with disdain, Marie knew why. They had the file from her first pregnancy. As historian Michael Sedlack explains female deviancy, Marie would have been considered incorrigible. He writes, "Within the deviant female population itself, a further historical distinction has been made between 'redeemable' young women – courageous but unlucky girls guilty of perhaps a single mistake or possibly the victims of predatory men (the 'fallen woman' concept) – and 'unredeemable' women – hardened recidivists, older adolescents, or even prostitutes." Marie would definitely have been put in the second category.

If Marie was considered to be on the unredeemable side of the divide over the nature of sexually active girls, Linda Chalmers, by anyone's standard, was on the other. The story of how she got pregnant is the one that everyone wanted to hear, or at least said they did: the dreadful but morally comforting tale of the girl who had been taken in by a conniving young man.

When Linda met Teddy the saxophone player she was fourteen and he was eighteen. Though she looked old for her age, she'd had no experience with boys and certainly none with sex. When she started to menstruate her mother gave her a piece of cotton sheet wrapped around cotton balls. Today, Linda is amazed by such a Victorian response. "This was 1962, not 1890!" she says. When Teddy came along, she was flattered by his attention and thrilled to have a boyfriend. After innocent dating for a couple of months, she had to choose. "In the summer I went away and when I came back I found out he wanted to break off with me. He had been fooling around with a girlfriend of mine. She would sleep with him and I wouldn't. The deal was that to have him back I had to sleep with him. That got me hook, line, and sinker. I slept with him. First time, first boyfriend. That's how it happened. I was young, naïve, and stupid. I know that. I wasn't a slut. I wasn't running around sleeping with every Tom, Dick, and Harry. This was my first time, ever. And I got pregnant."

Most of the women I talked to were so anxious for me to understand that they had been good girls, it was obvious how guilty they had been made to feel back then. Many of them still feel the guilt. At one or two homes a sympathetic matron might have comforted Linda with the old clichés – that she had made a mistake and perhaps she could make up for it. But at the home on Stanley Street, there was not a single compassionate word – no counselling, no information, nothing. If a girl was having a particularly bad day she was allowed to sit on the balcony in the sun for a while. That was the extent of the kindness anyone received.

Every home was full of stories. At some there were sympathetic staff who listened to them. But, for the most part, the girls tended mainly to confide in each other or, like me, to no one at all. If I had not isolated myself so much I would have undoubtedly heard stories such as my own. Perhaps I would have met someone like Marie, someone else in agony over a true love lost. I could have at least listened to a Linda tell me about Teddy the saxophone player. But I didn't do much listening. There were aboriginal girls in my home whom I dismissed – and I am ashamed to say this – as stupid, because they were so shy and talked so little. They might well have had a story of rape or abuse, like Loretta's. Perhaps I would have met one of the girls who were ashamed because they had not been in love. Or a girl who had "slept around," but who didn't think she'd been promiscuous. Like Ellen M., who had just arrived from Liverpool and whose Beatles accent made her "flavour of the month." That attention was hard to resist, so she went along with it. The young man who got her pregnant was just one of several lovers, but her greatest shame was that it had been a casual affair. "I just thought I was a bad girl. I had known this guy very briefly. I met him through friends at a party. I went out with him a couple of times. That's all. It was like playing Russian roulette. It wasn't something that I ever thought would happen. It seems so naïve, I know, but that is the truth. I always thought that women got pregnant when they weren't married because they were in love and couldn't control themselves." She laughs ruefully, "To say I was sexually active would be an oxymoron. I was just on the receiving end of this act. It wasn't anything I participated in particularly. But clearly I didn't have a long relationship. I thought, This will really look like I am a loose young woman."

She was right, at least in her assessment of what others would think. Like me, she kept to herself and didn't make friends in the home. There was only one girl I did get to know slightly. Pam was quiet but serious; she seemed to me to be less giddy than the others. Occasionally we went for walks and talked. Mostly I encouraged her to go back to school when it was all over – I desperately clung to my university status as another mark of

have sex because I would get killed when I went home, if my dad found out. And here I goes out and fools around a little bit and gets pregnant. I'm a good girl, but who is going to believe me? That's the mentality I came from."

That mentality usually followed the girls beyond the maternity homes. It could hardly have been otherwise, as the concept of healthy sexuality even within marriage was just coming into consciousness in the mid-1960s. Even when the taboo against premarital sex began to lift, contemporary moralists did not want to be faced with the evidence of sexual experimentation. The 1961 book *Unmarried Mothers* quotes American sociologist Albert Ellis: "The same girl whose sex habits may be tolerantly viewed by her friends, associates and lovers while her stomach remains appropriately flattened may be in for the severest kind of censure once she begins to stock up on maternity dresses." Officially, a young girl's sexual development was supposed to lead only to the altar; abstinence was not presented as a choice but an obligation.

It is hard to imagine most girls who were hidden away in homes coming out without a distorted view of sexuality. Whether they were virgins or party girls, consenting or assaulted, to have been sexual – to have crossed the line into womanhood – only to be shamed and hidden away had to have profound effects. But these were esoteric concerns for those responsible for the care of unwed mothers. They were focused on her bulging belly for different reasons. The topic of sex may have been uncomfortable, but its product was definitely up for discussion. There was a baby coming. And everybody wanted to talk about that.

# 5

# "Planning for Baby"

*"Adoption has become more popular, the unmarried mother is more knowledgeable about it and, consequently, more accepting of relinquishment of her child to substitute parents who meet agency standards."*
– Report on Maternity Homes in Metropolitan Toronto, 1960

After a girl's name – or the half of it she was allowed to keep – the most important fact about her in any home for unwed mothers was her due date. You knew everyone's, everyone knew yours. There was an obsessive attention to the progress of every pregnancy. The girls talked constantly to each other or the staff about how the baby was moving, or what they would do when their water broke, or what to pack for the hospital. Down in the smoking room, there was endless talk of what to name the baby and whether you wanted a boy or a girl. Upstairs in the common room steel needles clacked incessantly as the girls knitted and crocheted baby clothes and blankets.

I didn't participate in any of the body or baby conversations. I didn't touch a knitting needle. There was a wardrobe room where you could borrow second-hand maternity clothes. I wouldn't go near it. I didn't want to have anything to do with pastel dresses or Peter Pan collars. I prided myself on a boutique dress I had splurged on – not a maternity dress but a loose, bright, flowered silky shift tied with a long ribbon at the nape of my neck and an open slash down the back. And I went back to wearing too much eye make-up. It was as if a small part of my pre-pregnant rebellion had begun to re-emerge.

We have a word now to describe these very different responses – both the intense interest in the baby and the determined intention to ignore it. Overworked as it is, I can think of no better: denial. Massive denial. And we each had our own ways of acting out that denial and avoiding the obvious reality. The girls in the smoking room were full of baby talk as if they were normal mothers-to-be; I was pretending nothing was happening. They ignored the fact they'd be giving up their babies; I ignored the evidence of my body. Here it was changing by the day. I was doing what a woman is at least partly made for, growing and carrying a baby that was mine, made of me. I would feel it kick, I would even watch my stomach change shape as a baby fist or foot moved across it, but emotionally I was completely detached.

If it is uncomfortable now to admit how dismissive I was of the other girls around me, it is much more difficult to write about how I regarded the new life I was at least physically nurturing. If I have any shame left about those nine months of my life it is that I went through them with such little feeling for this child – that I was so cold, so distant – so disassociated from a growing being. I know now that I was not by far the only girl to choose this form of denial. Pam G., who was at Our Lady of Mercy Home in Vancouver, describes how she managed her feelings. "The way I understand it now, having reconstructed my past many times, is that I was in a state of profound denial the whole time. I didn't connect with a real baby I would be giving up, and I didn't connect with myself having real feelings about it.

As time went on – as I progressed through what I now know as the Kubler–Ross stages of grief – I felt the pain I had previously shut out. She was never a real baby, that I could love, until much later, when she was irretrievably lost to me."

For me, survival meant jettisoning any feelings that might have weighed me down and held me back from simply having it over and done with. I was not going to join the others in childish illusions. I wasn't going to knit anything or even imagine what this baby might be like. I was just going to concentrate on getting through these months. There was no baby. I was just fat. I just wanted to be able to get into my old clothes again.

My way of "Planning for Baby" – as Dr. Benjamin Spock titled the first chapter of every mother's bible – was not to. But those who did plan and dream were perhaps avoiding another, even harsher reality. They would not be keeping these babies. Most, probably all, of them would be giving their children away. Otherwise, they wouldn't have been there. Why hide what you're going to show?

The question of what would happen to the child was settled for me very early. It would be put up for adoption. That was what I always told myself, as if it were the government's choice, not mine. I did not fight for or want anything else. Being a mother had never been a part of my fantasy life, so I did not feel a dream was being lost. And no one ever suggested that I might want to – or could – bring up a child on my own. Where was the necessary husband? What about my education? I would have asked the same questions myself. Career was not really a word in my vocabulary yet, but I had an idea I'd be doing something, whatever it might be. And I felt sure the child would go to a good home, that my preferences would be considered. When I talked to the social worker about the kind of family I would like, the values – religious, cultural, educational – that were important to me, I never doubted those arrangements would be made. In accepting adoption, I did not think I was doing anything noble or shameful. I was just doing what was done.

Even if a full menu of options had been presented to me, I would probably have chosen as I did, and not only because adoption made practical sense. I did not want to cause any trouble, and my decision made me a very good girl. I fit neatly into the plans of the day for unwed mothers. Ideas and theories about the best interest of the child and the mother had been in flux for a hundred years. But by the 1950s and 1960s, adoption was definitely the desired outcome, hopefully to be chosen voluntarily, otherwise to be heavily promoted.

The stated ideal of those who ran the earliest maternity homes – the evangelical women's groups and later the church organizations – was to keep mother and child together. The fallen woman was encouraged to find a way to leave the home with her child, most often by going into domestic service. That she should first be concealed, then exposed, held a certain logic for these well-meaning Christians. As a single mother out in the world her sin would now be visible to all; that stigma and her new responsibilities to a child together should make her less inclined to waver. Michael Sedlack describes that early thinking in his 1983 article "Young Women and the City": "The responsibilities and obligations of raising a child, particularly if the woman remained single, customarily demanded such devotion and dedication that few women would have the energy, opportunity or inclination to repeat their earlier mistakes."

Encouragement for mother and child to stay together had official sanction and public approval well into the twentieth century. The alternative – putting illegitimate children into orphanages – was expensive for a state that had little interest in social services, especially to meet a need that arose out of a sinful sexual practice. Contemporary women's organizations also found orphanages repugnant. In 1931, Quebec feminist

Idola Saint-Jean suggested to a royal commission on social services not only that the single mother should keep her child "as a safeguard for her," but also to allow children to enjoy "the warmth and maternal care that no institution could provide."

There was another, more poignant reason to hope that mothers and children could stay together. It would be one way to reduce the disturbing number of infant deaths. At the Miséricorde Hospital in Montreal between 1929 and 1939, 37.7 per cent of the infants died in their first years, mostly from preventable diseases such as gastroenteritis or pulmonary infection. Women's reform groups of the time wanted mothers to keep their children so the babies could be breast-fed. A mother's milk might save a child.

But theory did not have much practical value. In reality, very few women were able to keep their children. Live-in domestic service – where a mother might be able to keep her child with her – was a thing of the past by the 1930s and 1940s. There were few jobs for a woman that paid high enough wages for her to run a home by herself, and child care or day care was not even a concept. In Quebec, although the experts were recommending that mothers keep their babies, either for their own or the child's welfare, only 14.6 per cent of *filles-mères* actually did leave the hospital with their child. The babies left behind had few takers in the Depression and war years, and they ended up in huge orphanages run by religious orders. Some of them became the infamous Duplessis children, orphans who were reclassified as mentally retarded so that the institutions that housed them could apply for the higher subsidies the government gave to psychiatric patients.

Perhaps the easiest period for unwed mothers who wanted to keep their children was during the Second World War. Though a woman's story would be scoffed at by many in private, she could call herself a war widow and a half-blind eye would be turned.

Because the wartime economy provided new and lucrative opportunities for employment, as well as day-care facilities, an unmarried mother had a much better chance of keeping and caring for her child.

After the war, a new dynamic came into play. Most homes continued to have nurseries where a mother could tend her child after delivery, but this was considered a temporary arrangement until the child could be placed for adoption. The girl had to stay in the home six or eight weeks after the birth, not to learn how to be a mother, but rather to make the decision about her child's future. In 1957, the Canadian Welfare Council said it was "a common practice to require the unmarried mother to care for her own child, because it is believed that only when a girl has actually cared for her baby can she realistically make up her mind whether or not to keep him." In effect, she was encouraged to bond with her baby so she could better give it up. This rather convoluted new idea had come from the professional social workers, who were determined that their theories about the future of the child should hold sway in the maternity homes, not the "sentimental and emotional" approaches they felt were still favoured by religious organizations.

As ever, the best of intentions were used to justify the new push for adoption. The old ideal was now seen as enforced motherhood. The modern answer – adoption – had advantages that could be seen in many, if somewhat contradictory, ways. According to Michael Sedlack, "The social workers were especially disturbed by the policy of enforced motherhood, which they were convinced undermined whatever opportunities the residents of a Home might ever have for further education or economic independence. They maintained that it was necessary for the young women to be unencumbered and able to relocate, which were impossible if they continued to care for their babies."

Other sociologists, such as Regina Kunzel, claim the move to adoption was the result of a new, less flattering assessment of the unmarried mother. Although the professionals may have had a theoretical commitment to the idea that each mother presented a unique case with its own particular solution, nevertheless many of them, Kunzel writes, "believed that out-of-wedlock pregnancy disqualified women for proper motherhood. Social workers were more likely to favour adoption because they were less inclined than evangelical women to see those who bore children out of wedlock as fit mothers." Kunzel quotes from the advice a number of American social workers in the late 1940s and 1950s gave their colleagues to encourage unwed mothers to give up their babies. One said, "The majority of unmarried mothers are not strong, mature, well-adjusted people." Another claimed, "Unmarried mothers, with rare exceptions, are incapable of providing sustained care and security for their illegitimate babies."

There were other social realties in the postwar period that made adoption the perfect solution for both the authorities involved with the unmarried girl and the general public. Economically and socially it was more difficult than ever for an unmarried woman to keep her child. After their brief period in the work force during the war, women were sent back to hearth and home with a vengeance – and expected to stay there. Married women were routinely fired when they became pregnant and were not welcomed back after their children were born. What chance did a single, pregnant girl have to earn a living either before or after her baby arrived?

Yet there were more girls getting pregnant than ever, and many of them were middle-class girls. A convergence of morality and practicality ensued. With the supply of pedigree white babies came the demand. And the care supplied by a maternity home guaranteed a healthy product. Orphanages, where the children were raised till adulthood, were considered Victorian, and most of them closed. Adoption was progressive and became the fashion for many worthy couples who could not conceive or who genuinely wanted to give a child a better chance in life. It also, unfortunately, became an easy way to acquire a child for some whose motives were considerably less lofty. The backgrounds of those wanting to adopt were not scrutinized as they are today, and all too often babies of unwed mothers went to violent, abusive, or neglectful parents.

In 1967, I could not observe my options from the distance I have now, nor did I have the tools to analyse the theories of the time that influenced the route I took. Recently, and quite by accident, I stumbled late one night on a 1950s movie that was the kind of cultural vehicle that helped deliver the message I had absorbed. *Our Very Own*, starring Ann Blyth, is the story of a young girl brought up in a loving, middle-class family – the mother is played by Jane Wyatt, who would later land the role of Margaret, Robert Young's wife, in the television series "Father Knows Best." When the daughter finds out she is adopted, she wants to meet her "real mother." She finds a frowsy, chain-smoking bleach blonde who lives on the wrong side of the tracks. The advantages of adoption are made dramatically obvious. What unwed mother could deny her child the opportunity of a loving, middle-class upbringing, which she could secure by just signing those papers.

My own denial neatly dovetailed with the lack of any other options presented by either the authorities or the popular culture of the day. Together they determined my and this child's future – or fate. But there was, I think, still another factor. By agreeing to adoption, in some cases embracing it, unwed mothers were signalling our understanding of the moral order and our wish to follow it. Having clearly flouted the rules once, we were relieved to now be doing something that was so obviously right. What could signal more strongly our reattachment to contemporary mores than to give our baby a good home with two loving parents? Adoption was one way to make up for our sin, and many birth mothers clearly understood that giving up the baby was part of their penance. One woman told the matron in her Vancouver home, "The adoptive mother will never have to worry about me hunting the baby down because I have to pay the price for doing this terrible thing."

As for our own emotions, everyone assured us we could put the past behind us and get on with our lives. No one would ever have to know. Although it was a sin to have sex and get pregnant, apparently God wouldn't mind if we lied about having had a baby and where we had been for the last few months. The message we got was: Don't tell. Just put it out of your mind. Soon we would be as right as rain. I have kept a letter my mother wrote me that spring in 1967 after she had asked a psychiatrist how this might affect me. "This doctor has advised girls before and he knows what he's talking about," she wrote. "He says he hasn't found girls suffering any after problems, and are only filled with tremendous happy relief when it's all over." Of course, he was right for many of us. There was relief at the idea of being able to go on as if none of this had happened. We were focused on our own futures, and we didn't want to be saddled with a baby we hadn't planned for. And we were convinced, by and with everyone else, that we would just get on with our lives.

At Sterling, Karin had planned on adoption and was going to stick to it. "From the beginning, I bought the bill of goods that the child would be better off in a family that could provide for it and give it two loving parents," she says. There was no Bill to help her any more, and how could she bring a baby back to a neighbourhood that had already condemned her family? She shrank in shame every time she thought about her little sister,

Ani, crying that her friends said they couldn't play with her any more because of "what Karin had done." And Karin was beginning to think about a future for herself. For a long time she had been fascinated by stories she had read about Warrendale, a new experimental treatment centre in Toronto for disturbed children. That's where she had wanted to work after high school. Her pregnancy had put off those plans for almost a year, but she still wanted to try. She knew where she was going when this was all over.

Karin managed her feelings very consciously and firmly. Early on, she absorbed the conventional wisdom that circulated in every home about how to cope if you were going to relinquish the baby. All the girls said, "If you don't look at it, you won't feel anything." Karin knew what she would do – wouldn't do – when that time came. Up until then, whenever she wavered for a moment, she would repeat the "It's best for the child" incantation. "I had to be firm," she says. "It was a huge fear in me of letting go of that belief, because if I let go of that for a second it would be disastrous. What a can of worms that would have opened up. Because then I would have had to make other decisions, and in my own head I thought that would have been a decision for me, for the child." Another girl talks about managing her reluctant decision for adoption by repeating the Serenity Prayer over and over again, "God grant me the serenity to accept the things I cannot change, the courage to change the things I can, and the wisdom to know the difference."

While Karin didn't deny her pregnancy with nearly the same energy as some others did – or I did – she set very definite limits for herself. Anything that could make the growing foetus more real, she backed right off. She avoided anything that might trigger any maternal response. "I remember refusing to knit anything," she says. "This is a stupid thing that I've felt guilty about in later years and wondered if there was something wrong with me. At the time I thought, Why knit stuff for a baby that I'll never see, much less put on him? Now I think it would have been nice for him as he got older to have had a pair of booties that his biological mother knitted for him. However . . . I didn't."

Perhaps Karin recognizes her own doubts better in retrospect. But if she ever did wonder at the time about whether she was doing the right thing, it was a question that she didn't share with anyone, not even her best friend at Sterling, Judy. For Judy, Karin was the one who had it right; her own indecision was, she says, "wimpy." Judy knew everyone wanted her to give up the baby, and she tried to convince herself about adoption, but it went against all her feelings. "I always thought it was wrong to give up your child. I thought Karin was strong because she said, 'I know I'm doing the best thing for my child.' And I kept thinking, I wish I knew that."

Judy knew very little about what she wanted or what she was feeling, except for confusion. A few weeks earlier she had been hours away from the altar. She should be married and expecting, not unwed and knocked up. But now that she had been put away, nobody else seemed to be thinking about what might have been. Her parents wouldn't talk about the baby. Neither would Tom. He wrote about marriage but never mentioned their child. She was alone, and felt she did not really have any choice about the baby, except to do what everyone else thought was obvious.

Girls were told again and again that the future of their baby was their decision. "Every effort should be made to avoid hurrying her into a decision under strain of anxiety," the Canadian Welfare Council advised in 1957. In the homes, the official message was the same. Staff members from those times are scrupulous about saying they didn't try to influence a girl's decision. For Captain Jolly, neutrality was a point of honour. "I remember a discussion we had, that we would never, never – it was the policy of the Home – never tell a girl she should relinquish or she should keep. That was not ours to do. Ours was to point out the pros and the cons. The final decision had to be the girl's. Frankly, I don't think that would have been my place to do that, no matter how strongly I felt. If she invited me to help her with this, I would talk it out with her, but I would never tell a girl that she should give up her baby."

If ever there were a stacked deck, adoption had to be it. The Canadian Welfare Council went on to caution: "The mother should know that if she keeps her child she may be beset by many difficulties of which she can hardly be aware before experiencing them: she may be censured by relatives and neighbours; she will have, in all probably, acute difficulty in supporting herself and the child; she may jeopardize her opportunity for a marriage later on." Three years later, a review of policies for maternity homes in Metropolitan Toronto was explicit on the issue of adoption: "Social workers and others serving unmarried mothers have arrived, as a result of experience, at the conviction that adoption is the best plan for most illegitimate children as well as for most unmarried mothers. This does not disregard the unmarried mother's right of choice, but with more understanding of the complications of the problem, the caseworker is able to approach the situation more objectively and to help the unmarried mother arrive at a realistic decision."

Although each girl may have had a social worker, or she could "go" to someone in the home, counselling as we now know it was non-existent. Unless a girl could display a husband-to-be or a very sympathetic family, any discussion about the future usually led in one direction with one conclusion. This was true as late as 1969. Wendy G., who was at the Providence Creche in Calgary, told me, "Each of us saw a social worker once. The one I saw worked very hard to persuade me that it did not make sense to keep my child. A few of the girls decided to keep their babies, but usually only the ones who were still on close terms with the child's father. I do not remember any coercion, but in fact there were very few options in those days."

Annie C., who was in a Halifax home, remembers how a group of them were helped in their decision by being told to make a two-column list of what they could and couldn't provide for the baby. As she said, the Couldn't column was full – she couldn't provide financial security, she couldn't provide a home, she couldn't provide a father. In the Could column, all she could write was "give it love."

The subject of maternal love is another source of irony. According to social-work theory at the time, in order for a girl to make a decision about her child she had to develop a loving attitude to it. How else could she decide what was best for this baby? Sociologist Prudence Mors Rains points out in her study of several American maternity homes in the late 1960s that "one of the most difficult features for girls in making decisions about their babies was the fact that the arguments made both for and against any line of action were expressed in terms of a mother's natural feelings for her baby, and her motherly concern for her baby's welfare. True maternal love could mean keeping the child, but wasn't it also 'selfish and unmotherly' to sacrifice her baby's welfare and stable future by keeping an illegitimate child in a one-parent situation?" The right choice was not difficult to fathom. A former worker in a Regina Army home says, "I used to tell them that if giving up the baby was their choice, perhaps they loved it more by giving it up than by trying to keep it when they didn't have anything to keep it on. But that was only my way of thinking, of trying to help them." An unwed mother was encouraged to call on her highest maternal feelings in order to understand she should give up her child to another mother. What she was to do with all that love after her child was gone was not discussed.

Although each girl was presented with an apparent choice, any serious talk about options was usually a short one. There were a few girls whose families would take in the child, and marriages were always encouraged in the home – complete with a wedding cake and priest, minister, or Army officer ready to pronounce the vows – but adoption was by far the most common outcome. By 1950, 80 per cent of babies born in maternity homes were put up for adoption. Judy Graham couldn't summon the support or strength to resist. Reluctantly, she agreed that she had better join the crowd.

The point of relinquishing their babies was perhaps even worse for women in the 1950s. A decade later their counterparts were beginning to think about careers, or at least a job with some meaning. Although feminism was still in the womb, and there was not a lot of talk about what a woman could do, there were stirrings. As the 1960s progressed, new definitions of women's future that might include more than marriage and children began to take shape.

But in the 1950s, girls such as Janet Roberts, hidden away in the back part of an old house on Kennedy Road, had their most precious dreams shattered. These girls had grown up in an era that encouraged an intense desire for motherhood. Janet had trained as children's nurse in England. It was a way out of a bad family situation and a way of earning a living, but being a baby nurse was also a preparation for the future she imagined for herself as a mother. She loved children and planned on having lots of them. She was carrying a baby she knew she wanted, but because there was no man and no money, she wasn't going to be able to keep it. And that was definite. "If they heard at the home that you were talking about keeping your baby, you would get called into the office and talked to. 'Why are you thinking like this? You don't have any money. . . . You don't have this or that. You'd be doing a disservice to the child. It would be very thoughtless and selfish, if you ever thought that way.' All the conversations were 'You realize how lucky you're going to make some parents – a mother and father who haven't got children,' this type of thing. And 'What a great thing you're doing.'"

Adoption was always painted as a good deed by the mother, the gift of a rosy future for your child that you could not afford on your own. But usually the information about who the new parents were to be was nothing more than vague promises. The consideration shown to me by the social worker who discussed my preferences was rare. In Janet's home, girls used to listen at the wall that separated their quarters from the front office. "You could find out about people and where your baby was going. We were trying to find out, because nobody told you anything." Because they were kept so much in the dark – in 1957, Janet had no contact with any social services – it isn't surprising that the girls became suspicious, as Janet did, that there was something sinister going on. "I don't know how much money they got for those babies," she says. "I'd love to know."

Janet has no proof for her conjecture, but her conclusion is not uncommon. I have heard the same supposition from a number of women who got little or no information about the adopting parents, or who had their children removed from them abruptly and, they felt, mysteriously. There are rumours about a Montreal baby market that operated out of a major downtown hotel into the 1960s. But they are only rumours. It is certainly not unthinkable that babies may have been bought and sold. The Ideal Maternity Home in East Chester, Nova Scotia, is an obvious example – but that home was closed in 1945 because of the Butterbox Baby scandal, and government officials in all provinces became much more vigilant about adoption procedures. I have not found any private maternity homes run for profit after 1950. Although Molly Breen in St. John's ran her house privately, she received government subsidies for each girl, and adoptions went through Newfoundland Social Services. As for the church-run homes, it does not seem very likely, given their large contingent of religious volunteers, that they would be involved in black-market babies. Quite the opposite. As the Metropolitan Toronto maternity homes report of 1960 suggested when looking for reasons for the new influx of girls into homes, "New stricter legislation have restricted the opportunities for girls to make private or black market arrangements for their babies." It was suspected that girls who withdrew applications for a home or left suddenly had found some kind of access to a "gray market," which the report admitted probably did exist outside the home.

Even when adoptions were fully legal, girls were often misled about where their children were going. Audrey T. says, "Of course, they told me my child was going to be adopted by a doctor and his family. I think they must have told that to everybody. I still hold that against them." Audrey's child, she later discovered, was adopted by a woman who was an alcoholic and later killed herself. Another girl was assured that her child would go to the kind of large rural family that she had come from. The daughter she found many years later was brought up as an only child in downtown Vancouver. So secret was the adoption process, the girls grasped at any bits of information and even those had to be taken on faith. The only official document was the one on which they signed away their babies.

Faith was also a factor in the placement of the child by Social Services. Private not-for-profit adoptions, particularly within families, could be arranged and were legal, but both there and in the public system, background checks were often cursory, and many children went into homes that would never be approved today. The mothers of babies that were considered less desirable – native or "imperfect" babies – were never told their children would not likely be permanently placed, but would go through a series of foster homes. And every birth mother had to swear on oath that once she had made her decision she would never look for her child, ever.

"In the best interests of the child" is not a new invocation. It was how conventional wisdom was presented in the postwar years, too. Given the dominance of the nuclear family then, the advice for adoption was probably the most practical. But when matches were made without a birth mother's input – or against her wishes – knowing the advantages of adoption scarcely helped alleviate the pain of the coming loss. We were not all babies having babies. Janet was twenty, Karin eighteen, Judy and I both in our second year of university. Keeping our children would have been difficult for any one of us at that time, but with some encouragement and support – even just emotional – it could have been a workable option for the older girls who wanted to try. But little or no honest effort was made to find out what an unwed mother might truly want for herself and her child, and how that goal, whatever it was, could be achieved.

Loretta Fournier was a baby having a baby. And in the Misericordia Home in Edmonton she was the outcast of the outcasts. Not only was she part Métis, but her pregnancy was the result of rape – a "bad seed" was growing in this little girl. But Loretta was beginning to have feelings for her unborn child. It started when she was locked up in the reform school and tried to hurt herself. "When I threw myself down the stairs, I realized that my biggest fear was that I had hurt the baby," she says. "I realized that there was a life in me, and I became quite attached to my child. I connected to the child – because it was the baby and me against the world." The idea of keeping her child took hold. But Loretta soon found out such thoughts were literally unspeakable for a girl like her.

She often heard her friend Sherry and the other older girls planning ways to keep their babies. Loretta joined in. She could dream, too. She even chose a name, from an Irish folk story she was reading. The baby – she was sure it would be a girl – would be Shauna, "lucky." But when one of the Sisters heard that Loretta was talking about keeping her baby, she was ordered into the nun's office and told that if she ever said anything else on that subject, she would be sent back to the reform school. Right away.

Loretta stopped talking about keeping her baby, but she continued to think and fantasize. Maybe her family would let her keep it. Her older sister, Victoria, had "gotten in trouble," too, and her little boy had been brought up as a younger brother. But there would be nothing like that for Loretta. Though her father continued to be supportive, he wouldn't tolerate any baby talk. He only referred to "the crisis" and how everything would be back to normal again "after the crisis."

Sherry was very bold about her plans. She was "keeping," as the jargon went. No question. Her first plan was to marry Ken. She was sure he would come around. After all, he had visited a couple of times. She just had to wait until he realized that he should do the right thing. Sherry didn't know or much care if she loved Ken any more. But she did love her baby, and having a husband meant she could keep it.

She had a Plan B, too. If Ken wouldn't help, she'd do it on her own. Her reasoning made sense to her then. She was convinced her child was a boy, and she figured a boy would be better able to cope with the social stigma of illegitimacy. The way she saw it, a boy could fight back when he was called a bastard. A girl wouldn't have a chance.

Sherry informed her social worker of her plans. The worker said she might be able to keep the baby, but only if she went to work as a live-in mother's helper somewhere she could have a child with her. Sherry had been down the wage-home route just a few months before, when she was trying to make it on her own, and she wasn't going to do that again. She decided she had another option. "I was going to take my little boy back home," she says. "I was going to ride into Galahad on a white horse. The mentality of it is unbelievable now. But as a naïve nineteen-year-old from the sticks, of course I thought I just would go back there."

After having given up her first child, Marie Benoit had no intention of giving up a second, and she knew she faced a tough fight to be able to keep the baby. She didn't discuss her options with the nuns at Villa St-Michel. She knew what they thought of her. She tried to talk with the social worker who came every week to the home, but the worker didn't have any patience with what Marie wanted. Maybe she knew about Marie's record, or maybe it was just her professional confidence that she knew what was best. Each session with her was a battle. "She was not nice at all," Marie says. "I use to dread going into that little room with her. It was no bigger than eight by ten, and it seemed very crowded, but it also seemed very cold. I remember sitting across the desk from her. She always wanted me to sign adoption papers, every time that I would meet her. She would say, 'It would be in your best interest to do that. You just can't go on, there is no support. You can't make it.' There was never any encouragement. And I said, 'No, I am not going to sign those papers.' And I kept saying no every week."

With Marie insistent on keeping the child, the social worker finally laid down some rules. Marie would have to prove that she had a layette for the child – crib, blankets, clothes, all the basics – and letters from a landlord and an employer to prove she had a place to live and a job. These were the requirements Marie had to meet before she could take her baby home. As Marie now says, "It is hard to imagine a married woman being presented with the same demands. With a wedding ring, you could have an unemployed husband and no running water." Marie at twenty and with several years' experience in the work force had to demonstrate to the state that despite her lack of marriage license, she could be a fit mother.

Perhaps Linda Chalmers, in English Montreal, had the loneliest time of all. Not only was she young and ignorant about what was happening to her body, she was too frightened to make friends. There was nobody in whom to confide her fears or worries or hopes. Girls from other homes who badly wanted their babies could plot, as Jean D. says they did in the Burnaby United Church home, about how, even if adoption were the rule, after they "got out" they would try to find their babies somehow. For those who chose not to think about the future, the other girls could still be a comfort. Pat D., who was at Grace Haven in Montreal the very same year that Linda felt so alone at the Catholic Services Home on Stanley Street, describes the support and warmth that she found with other girls. "I think most of us tried to stay away from our feelings. I don't think anyone really wanted to sit down and discuss the babies or what was going to happen when they gave these babies up. We tried to live like we were all at home, and we were all sisters, and we would try to cheer each other up."

But after the mentally disturbed girl in the next bed attacked her, Linda was afraid of the other residents. Her mother was in charge of all the arrangements and didn't tell Linda her plans. No one else ever spoke to Linda about what would happen to the baby. She never saw a social worker. The only time it would hit her that she was having a baby was when she went to the hospital for checkups. And even then there was no talk of birth or babies. "I remember just sitting in the clinic, alone," she says. "It was amazing when I think about it. Nobody tried to help, nobody asked any questions – Why are you here? What are you gong to do? – all the questions that would seem so normal."

The girls at Molly Breen's were close. The atmosphere in the ramshackle house was so relaxed that it was easy to feel that you were among friends there. Even Molly seemed like a friend to the girls. But, although she was warm and loving, she didn't get involved in the girls' decisions. She says now, "It used to kill me when they gave them up. I would have taken in all those little babies myself, but of course it wasn't mine to say so. Who was I to judge?" Nevertheless, it might have helped Beth to be able to talk to someone, as she hadn't even accepted her pregnancy, let alone the coming child. Although she could laugh and chat with the other girls about mundane things, she was too embarrassed to tell her own story. She didn't think they would believe that she hadn't had sex, and she couldn't believe that she was really having a baby.

Beth had no plans for the future even when she belatedly accepted that her swollen stomach meant she was pregnant. She thought she would like to keep the baby, but how to do so seemed impossible. It was not uncommon, particularly in the outports, for girls in Newfoundland who did have babies out of wedlock to keep their children – at least in the family. Another St. John's girl told me how she took her baby home as a new sister. In Winnipeg, Audrey M. and her mother were pregnant at the same time; her mother managed to pass both babies off as twins. Beth's mother was also pregnant at the same time as her daughter, but they knew they could never fool Dad. Beth could not bring a baby back to Portugal Cove herself. There, being an unmarried girl with a baby would just cause idle tongues to gossip. Beth was in a fog – she had no idea what she would do.

I found in interviewing these women who were unwed and pregnant during the 1950s and 1960s that the matter of adoption and how it was presented raised the greatest anger. I heard over and over again, "It wasn't fair"; "All the decisions were made for me"; "You didn't have a chance." Many of the women feel that they were coerced into giving up their children, although, as one of them suggested, "Maybe that's paranoia." Or maybe we're not facing up to a truth we are ashamed of. Maybe some of us are unconsciously revising our histories, insisting we had no choice because we do not want to admit the unforgivable – that we voluntarily gave up our children.

But, at the same time, it does seem clear that the supposed free decision each girl had to make was not free at all. Not only the professionals but also the whole social environment made giving up her baby a foregone conclusion. Regardless of whether they truly believed that she and the child would benefit by adoption, most women felt they were pushed into that decision and dreaded the day of delivery and loss. Others like me might have looked differently at the end, focusing more on freedom than separation. But whatever fears or dreams of the future kept each of us awake at night, we still had a lot of days to get through. That was going to be a challenge for us all.

# 6

## *The Home Stretch*

*"Special treats, parties and other events, under the leadership*
*of the Program Director with resident planning committees,*
*should be a regular part of the program."*
– Report on Maternity Homes in Metropolitan Toronto, 1960

At last, it was down to the final weeks – the home stretch – and what an enormous difference there was between this stage of a "normal" pregnancy and that of a girl expecting her child in a home for unwed mothers. A married mother was usually part of a loving couple waiting impatiently for the imminent arrival of "their" child. An unwed mother was alone, fearful and anxious, looking forward only to when it would all be over, and wondering what to do then.

The girls had to find some way to pass the leaden time that wound down to their delivery. And their deliverance. For most, their sentence – for that is how it felt – in the homes was three months. That's a lot of time to pass in a place that is not your own home, where you do not have family or familiar friends, where you have very few of your own things, and where time and troubles can hang heavy, unbroken by baby showers, shopping and decorating for the new arrival, or fussing grand-parents-to-be.

Many homes provided only chores and chapel to take up the time. For some girls those duties were welcome; at least they gave a structure to the day. The cleaning, the dishwashing, the vegetable peeling made them feel useful, and the daily prayers provided important spiritual nourishment to a few. For those who resented the work and the religion, they provided something to rail against. Or, at the very least, to mark the time.

But there were still hours to pass each day. Even with an early ten o'clock lights out, the question remained: How to fill the time? There were the bells and line-ups for lunch and dinner. But the afternoons were usually free and so were the evenings. Then there were weekends and often some kind of holiday to be endured. What to do? How to keep your mind off the present, and the future?

What went on inside those old houses, those brick buildings shrouded in secrecy? Was it all tears? Was there anything to laugh about? What kind of a life did the home make for the girls or they make for themselves?

—

I went into Maywood in the middle of March. For the first weeks, I spent my time studying and writing term papers and exams. There was a schoolroom, but I don't remember anyone but me using it. I'm told there was a teacher who came in regularly, but I don't remember her, either. During my stint, I had the room all to myself, which was fine with me. I pounded away on an old Underwood, writing papers on intention and effect in the preface to lyrical ballads, or the use of food imagery in early Elizabethan drama – subjects as far removed from my present situation as I could manage. My professors sent my exams over to the home so I wouldn't lose any courses. One of the Army officers invigilated.

By May, that was all over. What was I going to do now? How to pass the time? My friend had returned to Calgary for the summer, so there were no more Sunday-afternoon escapes to visit him. As I had no other friends – no one in the city who knew where I was – there were no visitors to look forward to.

At the time, I was barely aware that, in fact, there were activities at Maywood. This is also true of many of the other homes. Much as in Victorian times, lady volunteers – good, upstanding married women – were attracted to the plight of unwed mothers, enthusiastically planning treats and outings for us. At a Calgary Salvation Army home, a group of doctors' wives used to drive the girls safely out of town to a ranch in Bragg Creek for a "good old-fashioned picnic." At Maywood, the auxiliary used donated tickets to take the girls out to shows – musicals and the Ice Capades were favourites.

The staff, too, was busy keeping the girls busy, at least they were supposed to be. The 1960 report on maternity homes in Metropolitan Toronto had criticized the lack of planned activities in the homes. Some of the specific suggestions the report made for making leisure hours more productive included: "crafts and handwork, opportunities to practice shorthand and typewriting and to develop new skills in beauty culture, dressmaking and other artistic pursuits. . . . Discussion groups covering topics of interest to the group – dating, employment opportunities, adoption, marriage and homemaking . . . and special talks on hygiene, etiquette, charm, etc."

No follow-up to these recommendations has been recorded, but presumably many of the homes tried to improve on the sing-alongs that had been the entertainment staple of most homes in the 1950s. Captain Jolly at Maywood told me she used to be at the home twelve hours a day. One year she organized a choir among the girls, and in the late 1960s she arranged private time once a week at the nearby Jewish Community Centre so the girls could swim. Other women have told me about the craft room downstairs, where they dubbed the crabby officer who doled out wool and other materials Mrs. Knit and Crotchit. By 1967 at Maywood there were regular lectures on prenatal care and visits by priests and pastors of various faiths.

I managed to miss or deliberately avoid all of it. If the talks were about babies or morals, I didn't want to hear them. I considered myself religious, but in my own way, and I did not want to hear what I assumed would be a sermon. Nor did I want to be herded to a show with a bunch of pregnant girls. As for crafts, all I could picture were the mosaic ashtrays and bad hats that came out of occupational therapy in mental hospitals. None of it was for me.

I did, however, develop my own hobby. I became obsessed with my fingernails. Perhaps because they were one of the few parts of my body that still felt normal. I filed and buffed and painted them constantly. In the evenings I would walk to a nearby drugstore where I would study cuticle removers and nail strengtheners, orange sticks and emery boards. I discovered the amazing range of implements for the care and nourishment of those ten little digits. Not to mention the mesmerizing rainbow of polishes to pick from. I could easily spend an hour deciding on a purchase.

The same drugstore was a destination for a lot of the other girls. They used to go down in groups, a huge waddling mass of them, for chocolate bars, cigarettes, and chips. I, of course, with my determination not to be one of them, was never part of the crowd. If I saw a group coming, I would hurry on, or if they were ahead, I would lag behind or wait till they had all left. I was like the kid who walks ten paces behind her parents, hoping that people will think she's alone. Of course, like a kid, I fooled no one, especially not the family that ran the drugstore. The place must have made a pile from the Maywood girls. Boomer's, it was called, Boomer's Drugs – an apt name for a place frequented by large groups of very large girls.

There may have been a certain Zen-ness to constantly painting and polishing small surfaces, but doing my nails could only fill up so much time, literally and spiritually. A turning point came one night while I was sitting in the common room reading. I was on a couch by myself. The other girls were crowded at one end of the room, giggling as usual, and, as usual, I was irritated by their silliness. My book was a collection of essays by the English poet Stephen Spender. I don't why I was reading it – now that my studies were over I'm sure I would have preferred a mystery or thriller. Probably I was trying to impress the others, or maybe myself. Nevertheless, I found myself going back to one phrase, over and over: "The essential fact of solitude." I have no idea now of the context – probably some existential musing – but the words struck me as a significant, literal truth that defined my sense of my life. I was alone. And not just then, that evening, in that room. Love and now pregnancy had left me only with myself. This was the "essential fact" I had to recognize and get used to. That was the way it was. That was the way it was going to be.

When I first talked to Karin Sorensen about how she passed the time at Sterling she said quickly, "Oh, it was fun." Fun? At first I found it hard to figure fun into an equation of hiding and shame. But fun, Karin explained, wasn't the craft room or the discussion groups on etiquette that the staff planned. Fun was what the girls invented for themselves in a kind of unacknowledged sisterhood, survival mechanisms they created to cope in a situation that was as sad as they could imagine. A Maywood girl from 1969, Laura M., remembers how much energy she used to put into trying to organize charades or getting everyone together to order out for pizza. "They used to say that 'Laura is the social convenor, she gets everyone organized.' I thought, Well, we're all here, why are we crying about it? You can't. You just have to do the best you can and get on with it, right? I tried to keep everybody cheerful, but sometimes it wore me down doing it."

Karin knew herself fairly well and how close to the surface pain and loss loomed. She felt the disgrace of Bill's denial of paternity, she knew how hard it was going to be to keep the resolve not to look at her baby when her time came. But she pushed those feelings aside with a determination not to be pulled down by the undertow of disgrace. As Karin put it in a note she sent me after our first meeting, "At Sterling, I felt safe, in the sense of safe from public scrutiny and local gossip and condemnation, not so much by my immediate and close peers but by the 'grown-ups.' I was in a setting where I was no longer a pariah, but one of a group of twenty or more girls in the same situation, where we could joke and in our own ways try to make light of – at best – a miserable situation. A bit like toughing it through an overlong canoe trip at camp, with wet weather and hordes of mosquitoes. There was a certain camaraderie spiced with lots of bravado. But some of it was genuine."

Karin took on the role of camp counsellor for her band of two, and Judy was grateful to follow. It was Karin's idea to get the love comics and make up their own dialogue. The game was fun, it made them laugh. They knew the director wouldn't approve, and smuggling the magazines into the home gave them the slight thrill of breaking the rules or at least disordering the atmosphere. The staff at maternity homes had always tried to keep out that kind of reading material. Regina Kunzel in her study of earlier American maternity homes says that "popular confessional magazines like *Real Love*, *Thrilling Love* and *Sweetheart Stories* drove maternity workers to distraction.

Offended by the reading habits of one . . . resident, the matron told her 'about better reading being available' and advised her of 'the damage such trashy reading could do to her.'" Even the mildest forms of self-expression could get a girl into trouble for breaking the silliest of rules. When Karin and Judy snuck out the back door of the dormitory one winter evening to collapse on the new-fallen snow and make snow angels, Stevie and Robbie, the housekeepers, were shocked. "You girls aren't supposed to be out playing," they admonished. And, inevitably, "What about the baby?"

The health of the coming child could justify a hundred rules and many punishments. But the girls did want to play, not because they were young, and certainly not because they didn't care about the baby; it was more like an unconscious response to being treated like children themselves. What do kids do but test the limits? And if they got in trouble with a few old biddies – well, Karin and Judy already knew about being in trouble. Making snow angels came fairly low on the list of sins. So did smoking for the girls who got caught in the laundry room in the Salvation Army home in Montreal. One group of girls at Maywood played bridge constantly as their minor rebellion. They used to plunk themselves down in the lounge and play for hours. It wasn't officially against the rules, but the staff made it known to the residents who came after them that they didn't approve of those "awful girls" who didn't want to do anything but play cards.

Sometimes the trouble a girl got into was unintentional and the reaction much more hurtful. In Winnipeg in 1956, Audrey M. was just fifteen, the youngest girl who had ever been at Homeside. Her mother had brought her a new pair of black, patent-leather Mary Jane party shoes. Audrey was intensely proud of them, shining them every night for the next day. One morning as she came down the stairs for breakfast, she slipped. "I didn't fall because I grabbed the railing," she says, "but the slippery soles of the shoes caught the edge of the stairs. And the little major – I forget her name – she saw me slip. They watched me for days afterwards. They thought I was trying to abort my baby. And I was so offended to have people watching me like that. I said, 'I didn't do it. It was just a slip, you know.'"

At Sterling, the girls could get passes for an afternoon away from the home as long as they signed in and out and always went in twos. The buddy system was another rule for their protection. Karin and Judy got out whenever they could. One Sunday they caught a bus, planning to drop in on Karin's family for dinner. Her mother, who was so painfully aware of how the neighbours would judge her daughter, "flipped out," but the girls thought it was a great adventure. Another time they decided to spend a Saturday just like two ordinary married, pregnant women. Borrowing wedding rings from a box of fakes that the home kept, they set out for downtown Toronto to go Christmas shopping. They joked the whole way, with Karin telling Judy to stop gawking at everything or "everyone will know you're a hick from Kingston."

During the course of several months in a home, there was bound to be some kind of holiday to celebrate – or suffer through. Nancy K., who was also at Sterling, remembers a Halloween party. With a good sense of black humour, she wound herself up in a bedsheet and announced she was a "mummy." One woman who was at a Salvation Army home particularly remembers Thanksgiving. When she started her usual Monday task washing the dining-room floor, an officer ordered her *not* to do any work that day. For dinner that night the officers did all the preparation and served the girls. It was a generous gesture, but this girl also saw its flip side. If the officers were the servants today, what did that make the girls yesterday and tomorrow?

Karin and Judy spent the Christmas of 1964 in Sterling. This was the toughest holiday for the girls because of its associations with family, tradition, and, of course, children. The staff and volunteers wanted it to be a special time. Christmas pageants were a popular feature in some homes, with the girls performing for each other and perhaps the auxiliary or volunteers. At Maywood in 1969, Laura M., the "social convenor," proudly produced an Alvin and the Chipmunks routine. One year at the Salvation Army home in Calgary, the girls played popular songs on specimen bottles. And when it came to gift-giving, the girls found that they were perfect objects for Christian charity. Karin says, "It was really hard for me. At home we always celebrated on Christmas Eve and it was very modest. At Sterling, we were showered with gifts on Christmas morning. We got more stuff than I'd ever had. But it was embarrassing because it was all donated. We weren't poor people, but we got all this stuff. It was touching but a tad inappropriate."

Judy has a different memory of that Christmas. She was getting very near her delivery date and was having trouble keeping up a good front. "You could be friendly and into it, but after a while when you realized you were getting to the end, you couldn't any more." Salvation came when the director of the home pulled Judy and Karin off their housework duties to paint a Christmas mural. "I don't know why she singled me out," Judy says, "but they allowed me to take time off the general chores and I spent a month doing a full mural. All I did was paint those twenty feet of wall. That was a good thing. It was real therapy for me. I can't believe I did it, actually, but you can create things when you're really down. And I was, especially since Karin left during that time. She was sick for a while, and so I was really isolated. They published a picture of that mural in a church magazine. The director sent it to me later and wrote on the note, 'We'll never forget you.' "

The chance to paint the mural was the kind of gift that could almost make a home a home. But it didn't happen often enough, especially in the earlier years, when homes were more like warehouses for the wayward. Janet Roberts didn't spend Christmas in the Bethel Home in Scarborough, but she did mark her twenty-first birthday there. In those days, twenty-one was the legal age for everything and so that birthday was an important right of passage. Although the staff must have known her birthday from their records, there was no celebration – no cake, no gifts, nothing. It was just another day of household chores and Bible verses. "I felt very lonely, really alone. There was no TV, no radio. In the evenings we played board games or read." At the Bethel Home, card playing was forbidden, and in case the girls might have a yen to kick up their heels, so was dancing.

There was one anomaly. The previous owners of the home had built a makeshift bowling alley above the garage. It was still there in 1957, and the girls were allowed to play, but only once a week. Who knew what kind of sin knocking down ten pins might lead to? The Spartan atmosphere and petty restrictions of the home instilled an anger and resentment in Janet that still comes out. "I was very bitter about having to be in there. I hated the institutionalization of it. And the food. Porridge every morning for breakfast. Ugh. It was a prison, really, when you think about it. The sense of shame was awful. It's so hard to make people believe that now. It was awful."

Janet still tried her best. She had gone into the Bethel Home early in her pregnancy and knew she would be there for six long months. She tried to get to know the other girls, but the relationships she made were tenuous, friendships that grew out of the immediate need for companionship, not ones meant to last. And hanging over their heads was always the warning not to talk to each other about their past. Janet was closest to a wealthy girl from West Toronto and an older woman in her thirties from a farm in southern Ontario. Even though she visited them both after her child was born, she never told them her story or heard theirs. At the home, they provided companionship while they worked. "We all did a lot of work. We were sort of close in that way, that you just did it," Janet says. "You had no choice. You just did it. And you didn't answer back in those days."

At the same time Janet was keeping her thoughts to herself in Scarborough, Loretta was learning not to break any more rules at the Misericordia Home in Edmonton. Loretta wasn't the kind to answer back either, especially since she was only fourteen. She had the comfort of her friend, Sherry, and she had schoolwork to keep her busy. But she didn't limit herself to the correspondence lessons she received in the mail. She wanted to learn more. She wanted to read. She got up the nerve to sneak into the hospital waiting rooms in the main building and grab any magazines she could. She managed to find out where the nuns kept the schoolbooks for the older girls who were doing high-school courses and begged what she could. Anything would do. "I read French and English history. I was very interested in the Second World War because my father had been in the army and we were really close. I read every book you could read in school all over again, from *Moby Dick* to *Death of a Salesman*, the *National Geographic*. I had a marvellous vocabulary. I certainly have Métis blood, and I'm very proud of it. But it was very important for me to be educated, because I was going to be English like my grandmother. She had come from a civilized place. That meant to me that I was something."

There wasn't much else to do in the Misericordia Home. In 1956, there wasn't even the piano that arrived a few years later and with it the sing-alongs that were *de rigueur* in so many other places. The older girls could go for walks along the high bank of the river near the hospital, but when they did, the nuns would accuse them of going out to "flirt with the Chinaman" who ran the farmers' market on the flats below. When the home moved to new quarters a few years later, the girls still went to the river-bank for an escape. One 1965 resident told me, "On one occasion seven of us visited the annual bathtub race and sat in huge splendour on the banks of the Saskatchewan River – a sort of group 'fuck you'; a very relieving piece of acting out for which I was castigated and almost dismissed from the home."

In the 1950s, television made an early appearance at many homes, demonstrating its worth as a babysitter. At the Edmonton Misericordia, the television was in the room where everybody smoked and where, as in the dormitory, the windows were always covered. In a sense, so was the TV. Only certain programs were allowed. Perry Como was on the approved list, but the girls weren't allowed to watch any show featuring Elvis Presley, so they all missed "The Ed Sullivan Show" on the epochal Sunday night.

All the petty rules were too much for Sherry. Like me, she had lived on her own and wasn't used to a regimented atmosphere. But she had a lot more nerve than I ever had. And Sherry had Karin's minor rebellions beat by one of her country miles. Not only did this enterprising farm girl get herself out of the Catholic religious observances by an instant conversion to Presbyterianism, she was determined to have a good time. She planned a breakout when she heard that Bill Haley and the Comets were coming to Edmonton. Sherry and a group of other girls not only got out to the concert, they met some fellows there and finished off the night experimenting with marijuana. It's an adventure she still recounts with glee. "What a headline it would have made if we'd been caught: 'Unwed Mothers Overcome by Reefer Madness.'"

Sherry sustained her good spirits by keeping alive the dream that she was going to marry Ken and have a life on the farm with her husband and baby. Everything else was just passing time. That fantasy kept her going until Ken came for a visit just a few weeks before she was due. They went out to his car for their usual talk. But this time he really had something to say. He had met another girl and was going to marry her.

Sherry was devastated. As her carefully constructed future fell apart, her determination turned to frustration and anger. Until this time, she had been working with newborn babies up in the nursery. When her assignment was changed to tend the older ones, she couldn't handle the pressure. "I was in the year-old nursery now, and one girl had worked with these kids all of the time. The children cried when we came in because this was their way of getting attention. These were attention-deprived children. They were hungry for any kind of attention. They wanted to play, but we just wanted to feed them and get the hell out of there. One girl said, 'Just slap their face and they'll cry and then they'll swallow the food.' So I slapped this baby – the one and only time I have ever lifted my hand to a child. The nurse caught me. I didn't make up any excuses. I took responsibility for it."

Sherry wasn't allowed to be with the children any more. She was told to sew blocks for quilts. That's what she did for the last two weeks before her baby came. She sat at an old treadle Singer and wept her way through the final days.

She decided to tell her parents about her pregnancy at last. Now that Ken wasn't going to make things all right, she turned to her plan to bring her baby home to Galahad. She phoned her father at his store in town. Although they hadn't been in touch all those months, he had heard the rumours about what had happened to her. He had even gone after Ken. "My dad did the best he could. But my mother wore the pants," Sherry says. "My father was basically a very quiet, shy Norwegian, a patriarch, but still, my mother wore the pants. She didn't want to see me, so they didn't come and visit."

Sherry hated her hours at the sewing machine, but for Marie in Montreal it was the best thing about Villa St-Michel. She had no interest in any of the classes that were offered up in the craft room – the one ashtray she tried to make was a "monstrosity," she says – but there were several old Singers there and Marie decided to sew the clothes and blankets for the layette the social worker said she had to have in order to keep her baby. The problem was that she didn't have any money to buy fabric.

There were several older girls at St-Michel – nurses and teachers – who had had to quit their jobs when they got pregnant. At first they hadn't had any money, either. But in the way of the desperate, they'd found a way to get around the restrictions against pregnant women getting unemployment insurance. All you had to do, Marie quickly found out from the home's underground telegraph, was to get an address and be prepared to do some good acting. The neighbour who had given Marie the bus fare to get to La Miséricorde helped her jump the first hurdle, then the girls taught her how to do the rest. "You had to go in person to get the cheque. So the girls helped to bind up my stomach and find something to wear that would look good. Somebody lent me a sweater that I could carry on my arm. Then I had to practise walking so I wouldn't look like a duck. I'd practise walking up to the counter and leaning on the sweater so no one could tell I was pregnant. It worked. I got the money."

There were still a lot of girls in the home who didn't have any money. But they, too, got help – not from the nuns or the volunteers but from one of their own. "One of the girls was a teacher, from out of town somewhere," Marie says. "She was a beautiful girl, very outgoing, very motivated. She would go around to all the girls on the floor in the evening and ask them what they needed. Maybe you wanted toothpaste, or deodorant, or something like that. She would go out the next day and shoplift it! She said it was easy to do if you were pregnant because you had lots of room to hide things under your maternity clothes. Once she got caught, but the store just gave her a warning. Apparently that used to happen a lot to some of the girls. They would get caught and just be sent back. Maybe the store managers knew none of us had any money."

Marie, who had had such bad luck, felt that at last she was moving forward. By promising the Sisters she would pay later – she planned to take out a loan from a finance company regardless of the interest rate – she had escaped the order's frightening downtown home. Because she was determined to keep this child, she had a future to prepare for. She didn't have to find ways to pass the hours like the others did – she could stay all day up in the craft room sewing for her baby. After a while she got to know another girl who was also looking for a way to keep her child, and they talked about how they might be able to manage together. Marie would earn the money, the other girl would look after both children during the day. At least Marie had a goal, not the question mark that so many others faced when they thought about their future.

Linda Chalmers, hidden away in the Stanley Street home, had no plans to make for the future and nothing to occupy her in the present. Her mother visited occasionally, sitting rigidly for her allotted half-hour in the formal front room of the house. The girls were allowed out, but only to one café around the corner. Even so they had to wear headscarves and travel at least in twos. Linda used to tag along, and that's how she had her one adventure. One morning as the girls left the home for the coffee shop, they suddenly rebelled, *en masse*. "Why don't we go down the hill, instead of up?" declared one of them. "Let's go to Sherbrooke Street and over to Eaton's." It was an audacious plan that Linda would never have dared on her own. But she was swept along by the group, all of them scared but giggling as, for one hour of one morning, they gave themselves the gift of freedom.

That was the only time that Linda ever had any fun or felt close to any of the others. She was still afraid of most of the other girls. The only one she had much contact with was her partner for the nightly dish washing, but she didn't talk much and was often mean to Linda, calling her stupid if she put back a dish in the wrong place. Years later, Linda recognized her in the ladies room of a hotel in the Gatineaus. Although it had been drilled into them at the home that they were never to acknowledge anyone should they meet them after their "ordeal" was over, Linda couldn't imagine that secrecy would still be important so much later. Yet, when she introduced herself and said they'd been at Stanley Street together, the other woman abruptly walked away, refusing to acknowledge they had ever known each other.

Linda floated foggily through her last weeks. "I went from being this nice little girl in Hampstead to this pregnant girl in an unwed mothers' home. I was probably just stunned, but I can't remember much of anything. I can't remember the staff; I couldn't remember a face if I tried. I don't remember them being unkind. They weren't mean. There was just an emptiness, a nothingness, a terrible sense of being abandoned. I just didn't know what I was doing. Sometimes I try to think of how I was. I am not a stupid person, someone who doesn't ask questions. It was almost like I was a displaced person with no thought process. I guess I was just too young to know what was going on. Or what hit me." Linda continued, "You know, I told one of my cousins recently. She said, 'Why didn't you tell me? You could have come and lived with me and then we could have kept up with your education.'"

But in 1962 Linda's cousin didn't know. Nobody could know. She was effectively locked away until she could produce her baby. Most of the girls lived in isolation from the people they had been so close to just a while before. If they were in their home town, their parents might visit and, if they were very brave, take their daughter out to a safe place, where no one would know the family. There was usually a telephone at the home, but it was always out in a hallway, where everybody could hear your conversation. Girls developed codes for talking to their friends and relatives. Marlene K., who was at the Anglican–United home in Winnipeg in 1962, towards the end talked about her baby as a person named Lesley, whose plans for a trip to the city she would report to her mother and father, who shared a party line in the country. "Lesley think's she's going to be later than she planned." "Lesley arrived last night." A girl at Rosalie Hall in Scarborough came up with the bizarre metaphor of a lawn mower to talk on the phone about how the baby was doing. "The lawn mower is running smoothly today." "Yesterday the lawn mower was kicking up."

Then there was the mail. The morning mail ritual usually happened right after breakfast, a hold-your-breath time for anyone waiting for a word from the outside. The matron or Army officer would call out the first name of each lucky girl. Her last name would be blacked out on the envelope, to keep up the secrecy. Mailing out letters was often a complicated affair. When a girl from one of the Winnipeg homes wrote her parents, who didn't know where she really was or anything about her pregnancy, she routed the letters through a sympathetic aunt in Montreal, who would then mail them back to rural Manitoba with a Quebec postmark. A girl in Montreal accompanying another girl from the home to the post office noticed she hid the package she was mailing to her family back in Nova Scotia, because she didn't want anyone to see the address of her home town. The staff often colluded in these deceptions. At the homes operated by the Misericordia Sisters, mail could be routed through the mother house in Montreal to hide the girls' whereabouts.

In Portugal Cove, Beth Holmes' father was happy to believe she was off working somewhere. At least she was earning a living, he thought, so he never asked why she didn't write. Fortunately, he also didn't ask about her mother's trips into St. John's. When her mother did come to town, she felt welcome at Molly Breen's. Mrs. Holmes, who had already borne thirteen children, was pregnant again; mother and daughter had something in common. She and Beth both had a craving for strawberries that summer, and the two of them would go downtown scouring the markets for this treat.

In a way Beth was very happy at Molly's even though there weren't any programs or lectures or outings. When I asked Molly what the girls did all day, she looked a bit startled. "What did they do all day? Well, nothing, ducky, not really anything. Sometimes they'd lie out in the backyard on blankets, but really they did just whatever they wanted." Whatever made a girl feel a bit better was fine by Molly. If they wanted to loll around and read trashy magazines, why not? Who was she to say what they should or shouldn't do, or what was or wasn't good literature? Molly may have called them her girls, and she certainly loved mothering them, but she treated them like equals, the way she would want to be treated if she'd come up against a hard time. She smoked, so the girls could, too – anywhere in the house. If they wanted to go out on dates, "of course I let them – they needed a bit of fun," she says. And if one of the girls had a little extra money for something from the liquor store, Molly wasn't too bothered. "Oh, I remember they'd say, 'Now, Molly, come in out of the kitchen and have a drop,' and of course, my ducky, I would."

In some ways the days and nights at Molly Breen's were the happiest – and certainly the most secure – that Beth Holmes had ever known. "I didn't have much of a family to begin with, and Molly and the other girls became my family. We didn't really go into great detail about what got us there. At least I didn't. But I felt comfortable with the girls. And Molly was very supportive and caring. She gave you the things you needed when you are pregnant, especially, being so young, support, love, and acceptance. You don't need to be told that you are bad."

As for me, the days and nights just got more and more difficult. My sense of isolation came to a peak, ironically, when the little territory I had to myself was invaded. One evening, I went upstairs to find that my room now had a second occupant. There was a woman, probably in her thirties, unpacking her suitcase on the bed on the other side of my room. She was rough-looking, with badly dyed bright-red hair and harsh black roots. In my mind's eye was the cover of a *True Detective* magazine, with a beaten-down woman under a bare lightbulb in an empty room. I could barely say hello.

When we were in bed, she showed me the book she was reading. "Ever heard of this?" she asked. It wasn't a recommendation but an inquiry. She'd never heard of *Anne of Green Gables*, the novel she'd picked off the library shelf downstairs. As a child it had been my favourite book. Like a million Canadian girls, I had devoured the story of Anne and her adventures. In many ways I had fashioned myself after her. Though I was named for my grandmother Anne, I used to tell people I was named after the girl from Prince Edward Island. After all, I, too, had red hair and freckles, and my mother's family came from the Maritimes. As a kid I had emulated Anne – using big words, calling my friends "kindred spirits" and, once, in a fever of identification I had even tried to dye my hair raven black. Now here was this woman – this "harridan," as Anne would have called her – picking up *my* book as casually as if it had been a Harlequin romance. I was offended – and frightened. In some way I saw myself in her – what I really was, or what I might become.

The next day, as soon as I had finished my chores, I rushed for the pay phone and begged my social worker to find me some other place. Any other place. She did. It was with a family, she said, people who were "really different." I packed my bag, said goodbye to no one, and took my chances.

Living with a family usually meant working for them: cooking, cleaning, looking after their kids. But this *was* a different family. The Bursill-Halls had a friend who was a social worker and who they knew was always trying to place unwed mothers in wage homes. Geoffrey and Hilary decided they would like to take in a girl, but only on the condition that she would not work. She would have her own room, she could pay some room and board if she insisted, but it was not necessary. Anyone who came into their home was a guest.

And that's what I was. A guest in the home of this extraordinary couple who had emigrated from England after the Second World War. They lived at the very top of North Vancouver, on the last road before the rain forest began. Their house was not luxurious, but it was full of books and classical music. Dinner couldn't begin until after we had listened to James M. Minifee on "The World at Six" on CBC Radio. Our conversation was always about that day's news. The Six-Day War erupted in the

Middle East while I was there, and I remember excitedly discussing all the developments and their implications.

Geoffrey was the head of the linguistics department at the then very new Simon Fraser University, and I was impressed. In fact, it sent my academic pretensions right over the top. I got the idea that I would study Latin with him in the evenings. Kind man that he was, he actually encouraged me. In the mornings I sat at their grand piano until I'd learned Beethoven's "Fur Elise" by heart. And I read voraciously – *The Forsyte Saga*, C. P. Snow's *Strangers and Brothers* series about life at Cambridge and Oxford, and all of Thomas Hardy (without for a moment identifying with Tess of the d'Ubervilles). And when my brain started to hurt from reading serious literature, I relaxed with Eric Ambler, Dorothy L. Sayers, and any other spy and mystery novels I could find. I was in a home completely, utterly unlike the institution I had just left. The claustrophobia of the past few months disappeared. I could breathe again.

The Bursill-Halls prided themselves on their progressive attitudes. They called themselves Fabian Socialists, staunch defenders of free-thinking and women's rights. They often compared themselves to the great liberal couple of the Edwardian years, Sydney and Beatrice Webb. I was to call them by their first names, and for the first time in my life I saw a married couple openly affectionate with each other. Hilary always referred to Geoffrey extravagantly as "my lover and very best friend." I had never heard any adults in Etobicoke talk that way about their spouse. She shocked me more than I could have ever shocked her. She was interested in everything and always had an opinion. She kept a stack of stamped blank postcards by the radio to dash off her approval or disapproval of something she heard on the CBC. And public radio was new to me, too. In Etobicoke, the family radio was glued to the private station CFRB. All kinds of new ideas were sprouting in my head.

Good socialists both, they had no time for religion. After months of the Salvation Army's prayers and hymns, I doubled up – as much as you can eight months pregnant – one Saturday morning when Hilary opened the door to a duo of Jehovah's Witnesses. "Oh, my dears," she said quite sincerely, "I'm terribly sorry, but we're all atheists here. You'll have to try someplace else."

By that time, I felt like a member of the family and had become good friends with their two sons, aged fifteen and seventeen. I had come a distance since the day I arrived. Hilary recently wrote down her memory of that day for me: "I remember we served tea, and I felt you were used to handling 'tea time' in that English sense. I rather took the attitude that if *you* could put up with our rather unconventional family, we would be delighted to have you stay. But it was the teacup I remember. When I said, 'Would *you* like to stay?' you were so anxious to say yes that your teacup shook in your hand as you placed it in the saucer.

"I remember another thing. You and Damian went to a movie one night. Later I said to Damian, 'Were you embarrassed walking along with a very pregnant young lady?' And he said, 'No, Mum, I was proud to be with her.'"

This was the right place, and these were the right people for me. For the first time since I had gone into the Maywood Home for Girls, I felt normal. Of course, I wasn't. As soon as I left the Bursill-Halls house for a walk, I would hurry to the end of the road, where the woods began. I was still in hiding. Even there. Although these were the most generous of people, like my parents they never spoke about it (the baby) or him (the father). Neither did my doctor or social worker, except in the most clinical or businesslike of ways. So even those who didn't judge still didn't seem to know what to say or how to talk to us. A constant refrain from those who were unwed and pregnant in those times is "Nobody asked about me. Nobody wanted to talk about how I felt." Perhaps it sounds like a whine now, but then it was a need that was rarely ever met.

Even if there was little practice, there were certainly theories about counselling in those days – how every girl should be treated like an individual so she could come to her own understanding of what had happened to her and what she should do. The 1960 report on Metropolitan Toronto maternity homes recommended that "adequate provision for psychological and psychiatric services should be available to all Maternity Homes." But such services were not available to me or to anyone else I have interviewed. A skilled, non-judgemental professional to talk to, someone who would have seen through those paper-thin defences of mine, for example, would have made an enormous difference during those long months of waiting. But counselling in those times was limited to practical issues – finding a home to hide in and planning for adoption.

But by now at least it was almost over. There was only one last trauma to go.

# 7

# The Other Maternity Ward

*"I was a doctor at the Grace Hospital in 1967 in Vancouver, and when we used to come to examine the 'unwed mothers,' the nurse would pull a short half-curtain across her – right across her belly so you never saw her face. Amazing to think of now, but that was just the way it was done then."*
– Dr. S., Calgary, 1997

The maternity ward is the one happy place in a hospital, full of adorable babies, loving couples, and excited friends and relatives. Amidst so much illness and death, this is the place of joy. It's where the future begins.

It was different on the other maternity ward, where girls and women with no husbands were taken to have their babies. Once again we were hidden. As at the home, we had no last name. We were not mothers-to-be, but some other species. Or no species at all. For one brief blink we were mothers, then we were thrust back to being girls, bereft of a valid passport to either territory.

What is it like to endure hours of labour with no baby at the end of it all? With no one to hold your hand? No one pacing outside the delivery-room doors? If first admitting the pregnancy was a terrifying moment for every unwed mother, finally giving birth was the most painful time, in every way.

—

Perhaps if I had stayed at Maywood, checking into the Vancouver General Hospital on June 30, 1967, might have been easier. My contractions started during the night, and by 5 A.M. I was in agony and waking up Hilary and Geoffrey to take me to the hospital. At Admissions I had to explain that I was just Miss Petrie. No, there was no Mister. Yes, no family. No, it's just me. They weren't rude, just bureaucratic. I wasn't angry. I didn't think I had the right to be.

I was put in a room alone on the gynecological ward, as was the practice for unwed mothers. I had resisted learning anything about the birth or what would happen when I went into labour, so I was completely unprepared for the pain. I had no idea how to control it. I pushed and pushed at the buzzer, but no nurse came.

I was making so much noise – I could not help my screams and sobs – that another patient eventually came into my room, wanting to help. She was an older woman, in a hospital gown – there for some other "female" trouble, I supposed. Even though she was sympathetic, even angry that I wasn't getting any assistance, I was repelled by her. I was young, frightened, in pain, and abandoned among old women.

A few girls felt this segregation from married women in labour as a relief. Wendy G., who had her child in Calgary in 1969, says, "It was a kind policy to put unwed mothers in wards with women who were there for surgery, so that we were not in close contact with married women who were keeping their babies and getting visits from happy new fathers." For me, that protection felt like another punishment. Once more I was being put away somewhere secret because of my shameful condition.

Sometime later, an intern finally visited. Then it seemed as if I had no privacy as a steady stream of men in white coats came in to poke and prod and ask the same questions over and over. At one point, my own doctor swept in with a group of eager young students. Did I mind them being there, the doctor asked, while he did an examination? He wanted them to see a labour in progress. Caught off guard and feeling like a charity case, I said yes. I wish I hadn't.

The labour went painfully on and on. I had been there for more than fifteen hours when, quite suddenly, I was told that a Cesarean section would be necessary. I wasn't consulted, simply informed. I was relieved – partly because I just wanted to be anaesthetized, but mostly because I had stopped feeling like I was having a baby. This was different. This was surgery. I understood that. My only previous stay in a hospital had been to have my tonsils out. That was years earlier, but somehow I felt I was back on familiar ground.

I was rushed on a gurney through the tunnels underneath the Vancouver General and into a room full of bright lights and what seemed like dozens of people – all concentrated on me. Someone comforted me. The anaesthetist asked for permission to put me under. Although it was just a legal technicality, I felt I at last had some control, that what happened to me mattered to someone. Maybe these people liked me, or at least cared about me. For the first time since I had come into the hospital, I didn't feel that I was being judged any more.

In gathering the stories in this book I have tried to discover the positive aspects of being pregnant and unmarried because the contrary was so common and easy to find. As far as the homes went, there were good homes – or at least not-so-bad ones – or good people in not-so-good homes, or good friends among the girls who made up for a lot. But when it comes to the birth

experience for unwed mothers, I heard nothing good. It seems
that there was little relief from either the psychic or physical
pain.

In a few places, the staff from the home accompanied the girls
to the hospital. At Maywood, the Army prided itself on staying
with every one of its charges through their labour. One young
native girl wanted to name her baby Captain, after the officer
who looked after her. But Pat D., who was at the Grace Haven
in Montreal in 1963, says she was just dumped at the door. The
usual pattern when labour began – if the staff at the home
believed it was the real thing – was to send a girl off in a taxi on
her own to cope in an environment that was rarely welcoming. A
few of the women I spoke with have memories of a good doctor
or a thoughtful nurse. But mostly their stories are of loneliness,
fear, excruciating pain, and, of course, loss.

⁓

Karin knew all about labour, she thought. There was endless talk
about babies at Sterling, and she participated up to a point.
Someone was always having a baby, and she was both terrified
and fascinated by all the stories of labour. The breakfast table
would be full of news about who was having pains or who had
gone in last night. How hard was the labour? How long was it?
The girls became experts. Karin says, "I could have been a
midwife with that kind of training."

There was a tradition at Sterling of girls nearing their due date
volunteering to wash the long linoleum hall in the residence.
Everybody said it would bring on the contractions. And Karin
was down on her hands and knees, cleaning the floor, when her
pains started. She was relieved at the prospect that it would
all soon be over. But even though she had absorbed all the tales
about contractions, drugs, and dilations, she still wasn't prepared for the real thing. "At the home, although we talked about

labour all the time, nobody talked about childbirth. Did we have prenatal classes? No. Did we learn how to breathe? No. I don't remember learning any of those things, though maybe in those days – in 1965 – nobody had prenatal classes. I was left alone through most of my labour. It was pure fear and abandonment and a pathetic ignorance of what was happening to my body. I don't think married women would have been treated that way. The more I think about it, the more I think it was awful that we were left alone like that." The girl who had found so many ways to lighten her load in the last few months didn't have any tricks for this situation. "I just had to tough it out. There weren't any jokes now. There was no one to make jokes with. So there was no laughter at the end."

After the birth of her son, Karin rallied. She summoned up her energy not to hold her child, or feed it or love it, but to distance herself from him as much as she could. "I remember a nurse coming to my bed to say it was time to feed my baby. I said I wasn't going to. A moment later I heard her in the hall saying, 'That girl in there won't feed her baby!' I was protecting myself. But I did go down to the nursery. I went to the window, trying to guess which one might be it. I didn't ask because I didn't want to know, but I still speculated."

Karin knew the time was coming when she would have to know which was her child. "While I was still in the hospital, for legal purposes I had to identify him. I can remember the Children's Aid coming and the nurse bringing the baby out. They asked, 'Is this your baby?' I said yes, but I didn't look. And that was it." To get through the ordeal, she'd stuck to the rule she had learned from the other girls at Sterling.

Judy didn't have any of Karin's determined distance, nor the strength to "toughen herself up," as she puts it. The months in the home, thinking so much about the baby she was going to have to give up, had been bad enough. Having it was even worse. She went into Toronto Western Hospital at about 10 P.M., and like all the Sterling girls she was put in a regular maternity ward. The night that followed was sheer terror for her. "It was like going to hell. It was pitch dark, I remember that, and I could hear screams for hours and hours. There were a lot of women there, screaming at the top of their lungs. Everybody was screaming. I thought I was in some kind of war. I was terrified to listen.

"I was in pain, too, but I was just gritting my teeth because I don't know how to scream. I'd never learned how to scream. Nobody had ever yelled or raised their voices in my house. So the nurses gave me this thing to bite. And then this awful woman would come in to see how much I had dilated and I would think, Oh, please, God, let me have this baby before she shoves that thing in me one more time. In the morning a doctor came in and said, 'Oh, you're still here. I thought you would have had the baby hours ago.' So it was my entire fault again."

After she delivered, the terror subsided for Judy, but then the anguish set in. Now that she could see and touch this baby, her resolve to give it away made no sense any more. She knew she couldn't say so, but now she wanted her child – forever. "They kept bringing the baby to me, and I'd feed him, and I'd be crying and crying, and the nurses would come in and say, 'What's the matter with you!' And I'd say, 'Nothing.' I was in a ward with other new mothers, married ones, so that made it even worse."

Tom didn't visit, but Judy's parents did come down from Kingston to see their daughter and their new grandson. At one point it looked like she might be able to bring him home. Her mother said the baby was beautiful and she would talk to Judy's father about keeping him. But he was adamant it couldn't be done. Judy would have to go through with the original plan.

Judy, Karin, and I had our babies in the mid- and late 1960s. In the 1950s, unmarried, pregnant girls were treated with even less respect or dignity at the hospital. In Vancouver – in those pre-medicare days – girls were put into the welfare ward. In 1957, in Scarborough, Janet Roberts was used to the secretive way the girls were hustled to and from their doctors' appointments, but she was still shocked by the way she was treated at the hospital. She was put in a regular ward, but her secondary status was not in doubt. On the file kept at the end of her bed there was a note: "Do not talk to this patient." Janet's old anger wells up again as she remembers the hospital. "It was as if an unwed pregnancy were contagious. Those words were right on my file. I was nosy and that was one thing I did see. Then the labour was horrible, too, because I was really large. I had to have an anaesthetic. So I was put right out. I don't remember delivering. It was scary and I was all by myself. Girls nowadays don't know what it was like."

In the 1990s, new mothers don't stay in hospital for long. Neither did Janet in 1957. In those days, the usual stay for a married woman in the maternity ward was a week, or even two, so she could get used to feeding and caring for her baby. Janet was allowed to stay only for a couple of days. The hospital didn't want weeping unwed mothers to upset their other patients, so girls like Janet were promptly sent back to their maternity homes to recuperate. The babies went with them. Janet and her daughter would be together – for a while.

The hospital was not a new place for Loretta. It was part of the Misericordia complex in Edmonton, and Loretta had been there several times to filch magazines from the waiting rooms – and weekly for checkups. Long before her labour started, every Thursday she'd climb up the back stairs to be examined by a doctor, or, more usually, the student interns. The Misericordia was a teaching hospital, and these girls were perfect subjects. Loretta says, "There were three case rooms for unwed mothers and seven or eight interns. This one intern would say, 'Get up there and put your legs in the stirrups.' He would not say hello, good day, or anything. And then he'd say, 'Hurry up! We haven't got all day. How many more do they have out there?' In you would go, and each and every one of these students would give you an internal examination. They would talk about you just like you weren't there. In the third person. Very clinical. Everyone was able to get a feel, whether it was necessary or not. It terrified me. This happened once a week until the baby was born. I would be so sore afterwards. They would hurt you. And then you had to walk down all those stairs. You wanted to lie down, but you couldn't. You had to sit in a chair and wait until dinnertime or lunchtime or whatever. The worst was the humiliation of going in there. I used to think that half the interns in the city must have seen my bum."

Remarkably, there was one intern who was kind. While all the others saw Loretta as nothing more than an object to test their skills on, this young physician did see something in the terrified fourteen-year-old. "He is now a wonderful doctor in this city," she says. "He is the one person who said to me, 'You're a beautiful young woman. It is terrible what happened to you. And I really apologize for all of this. And you will go on and make a good life for yourself. You're a good kid.' He would seek me out. He helped me keep it together."

And there was still Sister Frances. From the first, she had been Loretta's lifesaver – her gift from God, Loretta thought – the Sister who was different from all the others at the home. It was to this woman – who never had and never would give birth herself – that Loretta went to when her labour began. She had not had any preparation, so she had no idea what was happening to her or what was to come over the next hours. But at least there was someone there. "I was terrified," she says, "and Sister Frances came to me. She asked if I had blood. She went out and got a pad, came back, and said, 'You go sit down, you're going to have your baby now.' She asked me how many pads I had on, and told me to put two on in case my water broke. I thought, What's your water? I was in a lot of pain all that day and all night. The next day they took me over to the labour room. I did not want to scream, but I thought that I was going to die. I was making an act of contrition because I thought that I was going to die. All of a sudden I was taken into this room and someone said, 'It won't be long.' Then someone put something on my face. That is all that I can remember."

The birth was not straightforward. For days afterwards no one would give Loretta any information about her baby. Finally, a hospital social worker came in to tell her it was a girl – but that was all she said. Loretta was too sick, the nuns said, to see her daughter. There were difficulties, an infection, then surgery. Six weeks went by and Loretta was still in the hospital and still wondering about her daughter. She wanted to ask her mother or father if she could take the baby home. But it was a pointless question. "I was too young to keep this child, and I was a ward of the court, anyway. So my mother came out and she signed the papers – the surrender documents. I saw what they wrote about me: 'Shows some intelligence.' That's what the nuns wrote. And the father? They said he was 'quick to temper.' That was how they described the man who raped me." Loretta never saw her baby.

Almost a month later, it was Sherry's turn to go to the hospital. She was frantic by the time her labour started on February 28 because she mistakenly believed 1957 was a leap year and that her baby would have a birthday only every four years. At the hospital, the unwed mothers were in a curtained-off area, hidden away from the other women in labour. Sherry decided to get up and walk around to ease her pain, but when she appeared at the nurses' station in the regular part of the ward, they looked at her in horror. It was "one of them" on the loose. She was quickly hustled back into the "other" delivery room.

Sherry was still convinced that the baby was going to be a boy, a son she could take back to Galahad. When she came out of the anaesthetic (using anaesthetics during birth seems to have been standard procedure at the Misericordia), she wouldn't believe the doctor who told her she had delivered a girl. She argued and insisted that it was a boy. They started laughing, she says, "like you would not believe."

Sherry was a fighter and she kept battling for her rights during her stay in the hospital. She didn't care what kind of trouble she caused. She was a fearless mother bear. "Remember, I was able to stand up enough for myself to use my own name. And I did it again in the hospital with the black pills. After we had our babies, we were given these round black pills that were to stop the milk from coming into your breasts. I would take them out from under my tongue after the nurse had given them to me and put them in the garbage, and then I would sneak my baby onto my breasts. Then they told me they weren't going to bring me my baby any more, so I stood there at the nursing station and stamped my feet – throwing a temper tantrum to end all temper tantrums. I told them that child was going to be mine for the ten days that I was in the hospital, and I was going to have her for each and every feeding. I wouldn't sign those papers if they did not comply."

Sherry still didn't think she would ever have to sign those papers. But when her parents finally visited, a decision came quickly. The three of them went down to the nursery and the baby was held up to the window. The first-time grandmother had only one thing to say: "I'll never have that bastard child under my roof. You got yourself into this mess; you get yourself out." It didn't look like Sherry would be going back to Galahad with her baby, after all. The matter was settled. Another child would be available for adoption.

Marie Benoit had a fight on her hands, too, just convincing the nuns at Villa St-Michel that she was ready to deliver. She was only seven months pregnant, but she'd had a child before and remembered what it was like. However, the nun she woke up in the middle of the night was sure that she knew better. "I knocked on her door, and I said, 'I'm in labour.' She said, 'You can't be, you're only seven months pregnant.' And I said, 'I'm in labour, I know I'm in labour.' She just ordered me to go back to my room. I was crying and I told my roommate that I was going to have a baby. She said, 'We'll have to go back.' We went back. The nun still didn't want to believe me, but when she saw I was having contractions, and they were getting really close, she got scared and drove me to La Miséricorde downtown, where everybody went for delivery. After I got there it didn't take very long. I got a call the next day from the nun. She asked me what I did to try and have my baby. She was suggesting I did something to induce it."

Because this was her second illegitimate child, Marie was under constant suspicion, and both spoken and unspoken criticism. "Accusing me of trying to induce the baby was bad enough," she says, "but it was worse during that week at the hospital because I was made to feel ashamed. The nuns' attitude was 'Oh, that's her second one, so that's even worse.'"

It was not just the repeaters who got the cold shoulder from the nuns at the hospital. Marie was in a separate ward with the other unwed mothers and all of them were treated as if they were a burden on the hospital's facilities. "There were six or eight of us," she says. "One particular girl was really sick, and she was not getting the attention she should have. She would be crying. You would almost see a little smile on the nuns' faces. I don't remember exactly what they said, but I can still see those little smirks on their faces. The tone of voice that made me feel I was no good. I deserved what I was getting. Someone told me not too long ago that a nun was talking to someone about how the girls did not get any pain relief. The nun said with a little smile, 'We purposely did that.' "

Marie says she got no help with pain. Other girls, particularly in the 1950s, say they were knocked out completely. Were they all treated so differently from married women? Certainly, childbirth in those decades was not the natural, participatory event that it can be today. But these stories from thirty and forty years ago probably describe more than just the emotional pain of abandonment and loneliness. The Montreal Miséricorde of the early 1950s has been described by historian Marie-Paul Malovin as a very large laboratory "where the *filles-mères* were the guinea pigs of these doctors and the doctors in training." A former manager of nursing at a Newfoundland hospital told me of a head nurse under her supervision who refused to give equal treatment to unmarried mothers on her ward well into the 1980s. Unmarried mothers experienced in the hospital exactly what they had found in the outside world – judgement. A study published in the *International Journal of Group Psychotherapy* in 1967 reported, "Unwed mothers felt that the clinic nurses and doctors treated them differently than other patients. They also expressed that they were afraid that the doctor would be punitive."

No one I talked to remembers the needs of an unmarried mother being taken into account by the hospitals. Quite the contrary. Not only were these girls and young women study material for students, they were sometimes used to test new medical procedures or drugs. Jean D. told me about the way she was treated at the Vancouver General. "It was at the time when they were beginning to say that X-rays were not good for pregnant women. And I remember being X-rayed and X-rayed and X-rayed like we were real guinea pigs. I don't remember having the baby, but the next day a doctor (or a man in a suit) came to my bed and asked me what I could remember. He told me that they had used an experimental drug for childbirth, to see how much you could remember after. I told him I remembered being scared, that I thought I was going to die. I can't swear he literally used the word experimental, but it was to that effect. They were trying something different, but he made out it was to make it less painful or easier to have a baby. All he wanted to know was what I remembered, and I didn't remember anything."

Marie was keeping her baby girl, but because she was premature Marie wasn't allowed to hold her, just to watch her through the glass in the nursery. The other girls from her ward would come down to stare through the window, too. "You would write your name, or at least your fake name, on a piece of paper and hold it up to the window for the nurse and show it to her, and she would bring the little crib. They would only leave the baby there for five minutes, at the very most. And you would hear some cries. It was the mothers. The birth mothers would be crying. They had been advised by Social Services not to go and see their babies because they had already signed the adoption papers. But they still wanted to see them, even though they knew the babies would be going. That was the most pitiful thing to hear. I knew that I was keeping my daughter. We weren't going to be separated. But I could just feel their pain."

Linda Chalmers, the fifteen-year-old English Catholic girl, was much like one of those girls gathered around the window at La Miséricorde. But this was a different hospital, the Catherine Booth Hospital in Montreal run by the Salvation Army, and Linda wasn't crying. She didn't have enough feeling left to weep or even to understand what had happened to her. Her labour had started in the middle of the night and she was left alone from the first pain. "I'll never forget this. I was given this taxi voucher. It was probably three o'clock in the morning. The bag that had been pre-packed was ready. They put me in a taxi by myself and sent me off to the hospital. Nobody went with me. I went into labour with a little bit of ether. Just enough to make me feel drowsy."

Linda had no emotions before or after the birth for the child she had carried for so many months. But in the regular maternity ward, surrounded by other happy mothers with their new babies and exuberant husbands, Linda knew she was different, and she didn't want to be. Like a kid, she pretended. "There were probably ten women. The wards were quite large then. Anybody who knows me knows I'm not a liar, but I'm sure I must have told them a lie. I can't imagine telling them I was giving the baby up for adoption. Maybe I said the baby was sick. I remember sneaking down to the nursery. I was told I was not allowed to see the baby, but I did see him. I showed them the name on my bracelet, and somebody messed up or felt sorry for me. I remember thinking he looked like Teddy."

Linda Chalmers was a Catholic who ended up at a Protestant hospital. In St. John's, Beth Holmes was a Protestant who ended up at the Catholic hospital. Most of the unwed mothers there went to the Salvation Army's Grace Hospital, but she was sent without any consultation to St. Clare's. After the warmth and acceptance of Molly's, this was a new and alienating environment. "I'm not Catholic," Beth says. "Not even a recovering Catholic. I was Anglican, and I wasn't used to nuns. I didn't even know what a Sister was, only what I'd seen on TV. I never had any exposure to them until I went into that particular hospital."

Beth was completely on her own now. Her mother couldn't

get away from her father to be with her, and the nuns gave her no comfort. "All these old women in these black robes, they just let me suffer. It was a nightmare, and I've never gotten over it. I was there two days in labour. I mean really, really bad labour. The nuns were there, and I've always said to myself that they must have been trying to punish me because I was unmarried. I should never have had her on my own. She was ten pounds, two ounces. I should have had a C-section, but nobody explained anything. I had no idea what was happening to my body. I really thought God was punishing me. Honest to God, I did, to have that kind of labour for so long."

After her baby was born, Beth felt more than just a lack of concern from the Sisters, more like an active disdain for her and girls like her. "When I think back, it was their whole attitude. I wasn't married. And they weren't at all sensitive. They didn't answer any questions that I had. I would cry for the baby because I was in for a week or so after she was born, but they said I wasn't allowed to see her. I don't think it was done for my protection. It was because I was giving her up for adoption, so I didn't have the right to see her."

One nun did take pity on Beth. "She was younger, but even she was probably close to middle-aged. She was the nice one, though I didn't see her very much. But she felt sorry for me and managed to get the baby into my room, but, my God, only for just a few seconds. That was all."

In Vancouver, I had the kind of medical treatment that Beth should have had. I did not have to go through a dangerous delivery like she did. When I woke up the next morning and struggled out of the fog of drugs, the first thing I focused on was a small Canadian flag stuck in a cupcake on the meal tray in front of me. It was July 1, 1967, and the country was celebrating its one-hundredth birthday. I didn't ask any questions and nobody told me the baby had actually been born late the night before. For years I thought I'd had a Centennial baby.

While Canada was celebrating a hundred years of history, I had no sense of my own momentous event. I am still surprised and often embarrassed at my own complete absence of feeling. I remember holding this child and wondering what would be the proper way to react. My mother came from Toronto. Numb to her feelings as well as my own, and not appreciating what she might be going through as a first-time grandmother who would not be able to be a grandmother, I flippantly told her to go down to the nursery and look at the baby. I think I said something facetious like, "It's really cute." It was an unintended cruelty, but a cruelty nevertheless. Perhaps it was a way of passing my pain to another. She didn't say anything. Even faced with the reality of a nursery and a baby, we could not talk about what had happened.

I continued to feel nothing, at least consciously. I signed the papers without any emotion. I had not cried since the night the father of this child had refused to accept any responsibility for it or me. But at the hospital I did finally break down. I had been in there almost two weeks because of an infection after the surgery. Now finally I would be getting out. I was sitting in bed putting on make-up and trying to glue on the false eyelashes I always wore. I was reconstructing my old self. When the doctor came in to say I would have to stay another day, the world fell apart. I started to cry and I couldn't stop for hours. But it wasn't about the baby, I said, it was those damn false eyelashes. Why couldn't I get them on properly? If there was any other reason to cry, it was already deeply buried.

# 8

## *Returning Home*

*"Separation from the child is rarely achieved without some qualms
and regrets, and besides needing her caseworker's support in
adjusting to her new status, [the unwed mother] may need help
in returning to school or securing employment, as well as
facing possible community criticism."*
– Social Planning Council of Metropolitan Toronto, 1960

For some girls, leaving the hospital was the end of the story. The
papers were signed, or in rare cases a girl left with her baby, and
it was all over. Or at least it was the official end.

For others, there was more. In the 1950s, most girls returned
to the homes to care for their babies. This gave them the opportunity, some authorities insisted, to make their final decisions.
"It is believed that only when a girl has actually cared for her
baby can she realistically make up her mind whether or not to
keep him," noted the Canadian Welfare Council in 1957. In
fact, as few women could practically consider keeping their
children, the time back at the home was usually a period of
waiting until the adoptive parents were ready to take their
new child. Until the 1960s, the Salvation Army required a
minimum six-month stay for a girl after delivery. In Montreal,

197

at La Miséricorde, a girl had to stay the same period to work off the cost of her confinement and delivery, as well as the adoption fee charged by the order. Andrée Lévesque discovered in her research that "depending on her behaviour she could earn good marks, which could shorten her stay by as much as two weeks, or bad marks, which had the opposite effect." Good marks could be earned by giving a blood transfusion to a child. But if a girl showed any favouritism for her own baby, her stay could be extended for weeks.

By the 1960s, adoption was universally promoted as the best choice for unmarried women, and most of the nurseries in the homes were closed in the recognition that caring for a baby a girl was going to lose could be very trying. The 1960 review of Metropolitan Toronto maternity homes noted that returning to the home with her child is "of dubious value for the girl who is ambivalent or who plans to surrender her child." Nevertheless, many girls came back to the homes anyway – alone – for at least a few days. They came to rest and recuperate or for one last visit with girls who had become friends or with staff they were attached to. This was the one place they could talk freely about what had happened – how long the labour went, how difficult it was, what the baby looked like, how they felt. Then, they hoped, it would be over.

That was how it was supposed to work. Restored to her former physical self, and secure that her secret would be safe with those who had concealed her, a girl could now put it all behind her and get on with her life. As if it could be that neat.

For some, time has brought a resolution of sorts. In the last twenty years the stigma of illegitimacy and unwed pregnancy has virtually disappeared, and stories of reunions with lost children are more and more common. In the winter of 1997, North America, if not the world, was seized by the story of Joni Mitchell's discovery of her birth child. But not all stories have this fairy-tale ending. Not all birth mothers are celebrities; not all birth daughters are cover girls. There are a lot of angry adoptees out there who don't understand why they were given away. Many birth mothers are still tortured by guilt and the promise they once made, often in a court of law, never to try to find their child. And then there are mothers and children who do not want to look, who want to keep the past well behind them.

But whatever choice they have made, what about all the time between then and now? Did the girls just walk away from the hospital or the home and pick up their lives again – go back to school or work as they were supposed to, now that it was all over? Despite the carefully planned coverup, did people guess? Did the girls still feel stigmatized even as social attitudes changed? Did they marry? Did they tell? Did they have other children? Did they ever meet the fathers again? And what of the fathers? Did they feel any pain or loss?

This chapter is an attempt to answer those questions at least for the women who have been the major characters in these previous pages. Was Karin able to keep on laughing? Did Judy get the white dress and big wedding, with all their friends and relatives that Tom had promised? What was to happen to a young girl like Loretta, already a ward of the court herself? Did her friend Sherry ever get back to Galahad? Marie was the only one who kept her baby. How did she manage on her own in the early 1960s, when single mothers were still a rarity? Did Linda ever find out the name of the home on Stanley Street and who really ran it? Was Beth ever able to tell her father what had happened? And what about me? How did I end up writing a book about all of us?

Karin delivered her baby in January 1965. After she had signed the papers, careful not to look at her child, she began to feel like her old self. But still, she didn't go home to her parents right away. She wanted to go back to Sterling first. "I had agreed to return to Sterling for a few days," she says. "I felt that I needed to. I guess, without knowing the word or the concept, I needed some closure. Closure with the home, staff, and friends that I'd made. And I had to have one last joke – my way of dealing with the pain, I suppose. I had gone to hospital in maternity clothes and had a girdle with me that I'd worn to hide my bulging stomach when I came into the home. At the hospital I stole a bunch of sanitary napkins and stuffed them into the girdle, so I looked enormously pregnant when I returned. A rather sad attempt at camp humour for a woman who had just become a mother. But that was how I coped."

Karin went on to work with disturbed children as she had planned. When I first interviewed her about those months at Sterling and then having to relinquish her baby, she was inclined to deny that the experience had any impact on her, and she still does not see it as a lasting trauma. But as we talked more, she realized that some of her actions and reactions in later years were probably related to having been an unwed mother. In her job, she always had many adoptive children to work with, far more than any of her colleagues. She had never given it much thought before, but now sees that it was not that there was a relationship between being adopted and being disturbed, as she had assumed, but because she wanted to take on these children, and volunteered to do so. Was she, she asks herself now, trying to work out her guilt, make amends for having given up her own child?

There was another memory. Karin married twice, but did not have a second child until 1980. Her reaction when she held this second baby makes her think now that the first birth had much more of an effect on her than she knew at the time. "When Mark was born, I shook so uncontrollably that I could not hold him.

There may have been medical reasons for that, but I've never heard of another mother having that problem. My husband and I had to hold him together. Later, when I had settled down, I asked the nurse to bring him to me. I sobbed unreasonably. At the time I thought it was from joy. Now I wonder if it was that simple an emotion."

Her emotions were just as complex when she saw Bill again, the putative father who had said the baby wasn't his. Soon after their baby was born, he phoned to apologize for having denied paternity. He had just started university in another city when Karin told him she was pregnant and had panicked because he thought Children's Aid would come after him for money. Over the years, he stayed in touch as he married and had several more children. Then one day in 1987, he showed up at Karin's door. She was divorced by that time; so was Bill. "It was quite strange," Karin says. "He was living out West, but had come to Toronto, and he just sort of dropped in with his three young children in tow. I was making dinner and said I could stretch it out – like the loaves and fishes, I guess – then we sat down. And there we all were at the very same table and I was thinking, Here are your kids and my kid, but ours is missing. I know that sounds sentimental, but it gave me a shiver.

"We talked about it afterwards. We'd both had that weird feeling – yours and mine, but not ours. He told me he had registered with the adoption finders and had brought a form for me to fill out in case our son wanted to find us. I think that was quite splendid of him. He had a lot of qualities like that that emerged when he was older."

That was the last time Karin saw Bill. A couple of years later her mother saw his obituary in the *Globe and Mail*. Karin doesn't know how he died.

Since her stroke in 1989, Karin has seen her life change dramatically. She and her sixteen-year-old son now live downstairs from her parents, whom she has to depend on for a lot of help. They are still a close family. I visited with Karin several times, and her mother often dropped in. While her daughter has a rather sanguine attitude to all that happened more than thirty years ago, Mrs. Sorensen remains angry. "I first refused to see the baby," she says, "because I felt this would make it so much harder to let him go. However, I did see him for a brief time in the nursery. Considering the times, I think it was the way, but I have never quite forgiven myself for not saying to hell with you all and keeping that baby. I still feel that society treated these girls in a most despicable way in those days. But, thankfully, times have changed, and there is no longer the need for the hiding and the lies."

Karin is not interested in finding her first child. Without going into it further, she simply says it would be too much responsibility. Oddly, for the girl who would admit to the least shame when she was hidden away, today she is inclined to keep her story private. "We were hidden away in 1965, and by 1970 hiding would have been almost laughable. But I fear the pendulum may be swinging back again. In the 1970s I would readily tell someone close about it, but today I would definitely think twice."

Until I approached her for this book, Karin had not told her son about that first pregnancy. Now she has. She wrote to me after our first conversation on the phone: "Your call prompted me to tell my son, Mark, that he had a brother that was thirty-one years old. I just felt like it was nonsense to keep it a secret any longer and to worry about talking about it in front of him. Mark's immediate reaction to the news was surprise and curiosity and then awe at the thought that he had a big brother out there somewhere in the world. He was completely non-judgemental, but then he's my kid and I've raised him."

Karin's friend Judy Graham is a lawyer today and the mother of four children. The oldest, Jeremy, is the baby born during the "night of terror" at Toronto Western Hospital. When Judy returned to Sterling, the director gave her the usual advice: " 'You just put this behind you and keep on going because you can do things.' But I didn't. I sunk back into it."

Judy couldn't bring herself to sign the final adoption papers. Jeremy was made a temporary ward of the court. For three months Judy visited him in a foster home trying to plan a future for the two of them. It came when Tom and she got finally got married. It wasn't a big wedding, and for the bride it was definitely off-white – she didn't know how much or even if she cared at all for Tom any more. But it was the only way she could keep her child. The marriage was not particularly successful, though they had several more children. Like Karin, Judy had another tragedy awaiting her. In 1982, Tom and their second child were both killed in a car accident.

Judy and Karin are still close friends – best friends – who have continued to see each other through their difficult times. One evening I met with them both over another bottle of wine at Karin's house in Toronto. I wanted the two of them to try to help me figure something out. Sterling had been such a beautiful place – everyone comments on how attractive it was. And no one there was outrightly cruel to the girls. Similarly, Maywood may have been plain and regimented, but no one said to my face that I was a sinner. So why do we all feel being put away in a home was so traumatic? I was afraid perhaps we just trying to "belong" in the 1990s by finding a role for ourselves as victims. That was a trap I didn't want to fall into.

Judy agrees that there was nothing wrong with the home, but says, "The fact that it was there and we were there was a put down. I remember the first time I went to a shrink I just blurted out, 'I was eighteen and they put me in this home for unwed mothers.' We were put there because we weren't supposed to have sex until we were married. The very fact that we had to be hidden away from public view implied that we had done something shameful. And we'd been caught at it – double shame! It wasn't in the Criminal Code, but we had broken a societal taboo that was almost as serious. Wasn't it only just that we should be hidden away? Weren't we only getting what we deserved?"

For Karin, part of the shame came, however indirectly, from the women who ran the homes. As she bluntly put it that evening, "Let's face it, they were a bunch of professional virgins. That was literally true for the nuns, and the others were Christians with a capital C who saw themselves as chaste within the bounds of wedlock. The very core of the religious life or practice which had brought them to this work was the denial and repression of their own sexuality. We were exactly what they were not, blatantly sexual – as they saw it – and now condemned by society. By looking after us they could feel both virtuous and superior at the same time. This didn't have to be directly communicated. But the message got through somehow, no matter how unwittingly."

Janet Roberts isn't the type to theorize about why having to hide out in a home for unwed mothers was such a scarring experience for her. She only has to remember what it was like when she came back to the Bethel Home after her daughter was born in 1957. There was no question of this being a time for her to "realistically make up her mind whether or not to keep her child." She knew there was no way she would be able to keep her daughter, but it was a requirement of the home that mothers fed and cared for their babies for several weeks. No one told Janet about what would happen next. "One morning I got up and the baby was gone," she said. "I guess I signed papers when I first went in there. I know that the people came from out of town. I knew that, but that's all I knew. The baby was gone. I withdrew then. I just clammed up. I didn't talk about anything. I wouldn't talk to anybody. I just took it all inside. I didn't do anything. I just did what I was told. I left when I was told to leave and went to a friend's house – her parents said I could come back there for a while – and we cried a lot. Eventually I went back to my aunt's house." Janet paused before adding, "You missed your baby silently. You just grieved. You grieved silently, but it took much, much longer, much longer because you couldn't talk about it. My aunt didn't want anyone to know, so we never talked about it."

Eventually Janet did pull out of her conscious grief. She found work as a private nanny for a wealthy Toronto family – English-trained girls were highly valued and she could make a good living. It was difficult to be around young children, and there were still a lot of tears for her. Not surprisingly, she wanted to find a husband and have a family as quickly as she could. "My aunt introduced me to this lady and her son and daughter who lived in the basement apartment, and I started going out with the son. I guess when you're really lonely like that, you sort of attach yourself to people, and it's not very good – not very good at all. So I got pregnant again, but he married me. We were together eight years and I had three children with him. And that was the end. No more marriages, nothing after that. Since 1968, I brought up my children myself."

As a single parent, Janet worked to support her family. For twenty-three years she was employed by Scarborough Social Services. Part of her caseload brought her, as a professional, back to a home for unwed mothers – not to the Pentecostal Bethel Home but to the Catholic Rosalie Hall – and a very different way of treating unmarried, pregnant girls. "I interviewed unwed mothers that arrived there. Ironic, actually. I used to interview them for subsidy. At Rosalie Hall, they could have their education and they could keep their babies. This was in the 1970s, when everything changed and things were more open."

Janet is retired now. Although she's in her early sixties, with her wavy brown hair and slim figure, she looks, and acts, a decade younger. A few years ago she got a motorcycle licence. She says that although she enjoys her new life thoroughly, she has never come to terms with the loss of her first child. When I first met Janet, she had already been searching for Laura for several years without any results. "I have a boyfriend in Toronto and he's dead against me finding her. He says, 'You did what you had to do. Leave well enough alone.' But how can people say that? You can't leave well enough alone; it's part of you. You only have to know if she's okay, and you have to justify your guilt a little bit. My guilt was giving her up, giving her away. I knew that I couldn't keep her. I had no money, no job, no nothing. But of course I wanted to keep her. I think every person wants to keep their child, especially when you're nearing twenty because you're a little bit maturer than in your teens."

Janet's boyfriend may have a few adjustments to make. Just before this book went to press she phoned me with the big news. She had just received a registered letter from the Government of Ontario. Her daughter was searching, too. Soon they would be reunited.

Janet never heard again from Laura's father. She says she has just "blocked him out." Nevertheless, she's kept an old Scarborough phone book, just in case. Rolf had a brother and sisters, and Janet thinks she could trace him through them. But she won't try until there's a good reason. "I always figured that if I found my daughter, if she wanted to find out who her father was, I would help her. Then he could face it."

For very different reasons, Loretta Fournier never wanted to find out what had happened to the man who had raped her and made her pregnant. It was what frightened her most when her daughter, Dorothea, located her after the death of her adoptive parents in 1987. How would this young woman feel about Loretta when she found out what kind of man her father had been? Nevertheless, Dorothea traced Jack and found his family anxious to help her out. She learned that, although he continued to have a problem with alcohol, which eventually killed him in a drunk-driving accident, he did have a fairly successful marriage and three more children. Dorothea has come to terms with that aspect of her birth; it is her birth mother and what happened to Loretta as a young girl that gives her the greatest pain. "The hardest thing for me is that I want to protect my mom," she says. "She is not what you think. She didn't make any choices here. All these things were done to her."

What was "done" to Loretta continued after she left the Misericordia Hospital. She went back to the home only for a few minutes to pick up her things. Loretta was not free to go on with her life. She still had a sentence to serve. The van with the bars on the window reappeared, and she was taken back to the Good Shepherd reform school to be locked up again. Amazingly, her determination to do something with her life stayed with her. Perhaps it was knowing that a few people – Sister Francis, the one intern at the clinic, and now a social worker – had showed her some humanity and believed she deserved a future. "I know it was hard for Sister Frances to let me go back to the Good Shepherd. But the social worker who went with me was a great person. You had to be a nurse to be a social worker in those days. When we got to the Good Shepherd, she gave me a pill that knocked me out. I slept until the following morning. I had to get up and go to mass, but she came back around 9:30 and gave me another pill. She could have said, 'Just take her away,' but I affected her in some way. She remained my social worker, and I wanted to be just like her. After how I had lived and what I had been though, I thought I could really help people. I had the knowledge. I needed something to hang on to, and that is what I grabbed."

Loretta did go on to be a social worker. She, too, had an unsuccessful first marriage, but her second marriage has been happy for many years, and she has had three more children. At fifty-four, she is serene and elegant, with the slightly pronounced Métis features that so marked her many years before. Although she has good reason to be bitter, especially towards the Catholic Church, she takes a larger view and has kept her faith. "I believed that God was trying. When I threw myself down the stairs at the Good Shepherd, I had lost faith. I thought God had forsaken me because of something that I had done. But I had a great devotion to the Blessed Mother. I believe that she heard me and took me away from all that was bad in my home. I had a clean bed, a bed that no one would come in with you. I think because of that I had a devotion to her, and I maintain that to this day."

Loretta still sees her friend Sherry from the Misericordia Home. Although they could not be more different, they have maintained their curious friendship. Sherry doesn't forgive easily. She is still a rebel, still angry at the people and the institutions that she feels robbed her of her youth and her child. Indeed, trying to correct the past became a passion for her after her birth daughter tracked her down in 1980. Until recently she worked tirelessly as a reunion volunteer, helping to bring mothers and their children together.

Sometimes that enthusiasm has backfired. When she found out that her birth daughter had also given up a child for adoption, Sherry was determined to find her grandchild. She did, but in the process she alienated her daughter, who didn't want to know anything about that part of her past. They haven't spoken to each other for several years. She and Ken also kept in touch, and only since she broke with her daughter has the relationship with him finally ended.

Sherry had a tough time from the moment she left the hospital. Two days later she met another man, and she married him quickly. They had two children, but he was another bad choice and years of violence followed. Sherry coped by drinking, and fell into a long and severe depression. She tried to kill herself several times and, as she says, she has been in "every psych ward in Alberta."

But, partly through her work with birth mothers and adoptees, she has managed to pull herself out of the self-destruction that ruled her life for so long. She still has no time for the Catholic Church, nor did she stay a Presbyterian, but she is an active Unitarian. Today, at fifty-eight, she's chipper, single, and lives in Edmonton. She drives a rusty old pickup truck and supports herself painting houses and doing odd renovation jobs. She did get back to Galahad, though never with her child. After her mother died, she went home to look after her sick and aging father.

Although Sherry still resents the treatment that she and the other girls received at the Misericordia Home, she saves her worst criticism for herself. No matter what was done to her she cannot forgive herself for what she feels she did to the babies at the home. "It's what happened with the children. I protected myself by not getting emotionally involved with them," she says. "There were lots of times that I could have sat down and rocked them, but instead I ran out for a cigarette. That was the biggest imprint that the home has had on my life. And now, having worked with so many adopted people, to find so many of them who have never bonded, it breaks my heart, because I was a part of that."

After Marie Benoit left La Miséricorde in Montreal, unlike Loretta, she did not maintain her Roman Catholic faith. She is now more comfortable at the Onward Gospel Evangelical Church in Montreal. She has been very open, she says, with her fellow church members about her past and believes they accept and support her. Looking back, she thinks she lost her trust in the Catholic Church even before she went into La Miséricorde. "It was when I was a kid, I think, and some nuns told me because my parents were separated I would turn out to be just like them," she says. "I thought, If this is what your Christian love is, you can keep it. I went to La Miséricorde because I had no other way. I did not know anything else. I always thought that if you were going to be a nun, it's because you want to help people and relieve misery. Well, then, why did they treat people the way that they did? It was so contrary to what they were supposed to be. They were supposed to be merciful, and yet they were so hard. I think that the Protestants – the girls who went to other homes – I know they had problems, too, but I think that the staff were a little more merciful. But some of the stories I heard from there were pretty bad, too. All and all, people were too busy judging others. Their Christianity left a lot to be desired."

Marie did manage to keep her child, but it was a hard struggle. For four months the social worker on her case strung out the various requirements for Marie to take her baby home. There was always something else: the layette was not complete; the list of babysitters that Marie submitted was unacceptable; she had to provide full-time care; she had to prove she had enough money to support herself and her child, but she couldn't work at two jobs. After a particularly bad session with her social worker – she had said there was no way Marie was going to get her daughter – a knock came at her apartment door. She looked through the peephole to see it was François, the father of her child.

It was the moment that Marie had dreamed of for months. But she didn't follow the script that she had written. "I didn't even open the door," she says. "But I could hear him saying, 'Please, I need to talk to you, I have been looking for you for months.' I was so upset I just said, 'Get out of my life. I am going to lose my daughter, and it is your fault.' He said that he'd been looking for me, that he loved me and wanted to marry me. I told him again to get out of my life. And then I didn't hear anything. He was crying. My girlfriend said I was crazy. 'You have been waiting for this guy and now he's come back and you're saying no. At least talk to him.' She sort of convinced me and I opened the door, but he wasn't there any more. I looked outside, and he was gone. And then the following day I met my husband."

Marie's story may sound melodramatic, but it was literally the next day that she met a man who wanted to take care of her – and her child. Marie accepted his proposal three weeks later, not out of love but because she knew that with a husband she could have her baby. It was not the best way to start a marriage, but it has lasted for over thirty years. They had their difficulties at first, but persevered, even taking in a foster child, about the same age as the first child she had lost. It was only then that she had the courage to tell her husband there had been another baby, but he supported her in a search to find him. She was eventually reunited with her son. He had spent his first six years in a orphanage, and as a consequence was so developmentally delayed that he did not learn to speak until he was eight years old. Although he was not one of the infamous Duplessis babies – the orphans that were classified by the Quebec government as mentally retarded – his placement in a home with very elderly adoptive parents did not help. Her anguish over the way her son was treated galvanized Marie into political activism. She has formed a bilingual group to push for greater access to adoption records in Quebec.

Although Linda Chalmers still lives in Montreal, she will not be joining Marie Benoit's group. After the birth of her son in the hospital nursery, she put him out of her mind. "I didn't think about the child at all then," she says. "I've thought about it many times since. But at the time, no. I think I was numb."

Linda had turned sixteen during her stay at the home on Stanley Street, but despite her youth she left the hospital with no direction and no advice. "Nobody came in and talked to me to say, 'Now you're leaving, here's what you need to know about birth control.' Nothing, nothing. That was the amazing thing. I just had to carry on with my life."

Linda tried to go back to school, but she soon dropped out. From there her life went "from pillar to post," she says. "I went to a business college to take typing and shorthand. In fact, I went to two. But I tuned out. I was hopeless. I was just hopeless. I didn't like typing. I didn't like shorthand. I didn't really like anything. I didn't know who I was. I didn't know what I wanted to do. I never had the opportunity to think about what I wanted to do. So I just went and got another job, and another job."

A few years later, Linda thought she had found a way out when she met a third-year medical student. As a girl who had little education, she thought he'd be her ticket. He was "my way to get away from this horrible backwards spin that I was never going to get out of. When I was introduced to him, I thought, He will be my salvation. I don't think I loved him, I just thought here's this person and all he cares about is whether I can cook. And all I cared about was being saved from myself, you know. I was eighteen years old. I ended up marrying him."

The marriage did not last, but it produced two children. The contrast between her relationship with her son and daughter, now both in their twenties, and her first child mystifies Linda. "I have my two children today whom I just absolutely adore. I have a wonderful, warm loving relationship with them. So it's hard to imagine I don't feel anything for that first boy except to hope that he's had a good life. It amazes me – my lack of interest. You sort of feel cold, like you're this cold person. But it's probably the best way – to blot it out. The memories are so horrible."

Linda doesn't feel that she needs to find out about her first child, although, she says, "I would not deny this person for one second anything they would want to know." But she has made one significant reconnection with the past. After her baby was born and it seemed to be all over, Linda and her mother never spoke of the subject again. Her mother's silence was a rejection that she could not forgive. Her mother is very old now, and in a nursing home. After Linda and I had begun to talk, on one of her weekly Sunday visits, she took her mother a list of questions that I had sent her about her time in the home, along with her written answers. She left the papers with her mother. When she arrived the following Sunday, her mother greeted her in tears. She said she had no idea Linda had been hurt so much and that she had always avoided talking about that time because she thought it was best to leave it alone, that it would be too painful for Linda to remember. For Linda, it had been a judgemental silence lasting more than thirty years. Finally breaking it has changed their relationship. "It's like I started to love her again," she says. "And I swear to God it lightened her load. It made her feel better. I'm not saying everything is wonderful now between us, but at last it's out there. And I'm not here any more just to please everybody because I got pregnant and had to be put away."

After she left the Roman Catholic hospital in St. John's and the coldness of the nursing Sisters there, Beth Holmes went straight back to the warmth of Molly Breen's. She had to recuperate. "I had so many stitches, I couldn't walk up the stairs or down. So Molly set up a bed for me on the main floor. Afterwards, I used to go back and visit because I felt like this was my family, but I couldn't do that after a while. Every time I would go back and see girls having their babies, I couldn't deal with it. Because my baby was gone."

Beth and her mother both wanted to keep the baby, but "there was Dad." So Beth agreed to put her daughter in a foundling home. "That's what they called foster homes then, can you believe that, in 1967?" Beth would visit whenever she could. The inevitable followed. "I got into a marriage as fast as I could because Social Services told me that if I was married I could have my daughter. So, of course, I hooked up with the first man who would fall for something like that. We got her and I passed her off as a foster child. It is all so funny when I look back at it all. I said, 'Dad, this is my foster child,' and meanwhile she is the spitting image of me. Mam called him Grandpoppy one night. 'What do you mean?' he says. And Mam said, 'That's Beth's own baby.'"

Her father said nothing more then and not a word since. Beth had managed to get safely married and that's all that mattered to him. But like so many hurried, desperate unions, it was doomed to fail. "It just spiralled down, and so many things were happening then I had to give her up." Beth was assured by Social Services that her daughter, Lisa, was adopted and was doing well. But when Lisa traced her mother in 1983, Beth found out they had lied. "She wasn't adopted, she was in a foster home," Beth says. "And she was physically, sexually, and emotionally abused till she was sixteen."

Beth had never told Lisa's father about his parenthood. She had been too embarrassed to face him, but her daughter had no qualms. "I told my daughter when she was nineteen years old. She kept asking and asking. I wanted no connection with him, you know. And I didn't think that she needed to know that bit about her roots. But I finally told her under a lot of pressure. She went to where he worked. 'Hello, Dad!' she says. She's brazen like that. Of course, he denied it. He said, 'I never, ever had sex with your mother. You're not mine.' But he invited her up to his home to meet his wife and three children. And after he looked at her and at his son – they've got the same face and eyes – he said, 'I don't know how you got here, but I guess you're mine.'"

Beth's daughter was an angry young woman and the mother she met was also having a rough time. A second marriage also didn't work. Beth's self-esteem was at rock bottom. When she ended up in a shelter for battered women, Beth decided it was time to get things right. Through courses and workshops, she got herself straightened around, then went to work for other people who needed help. Today, she's a counsellor in St. John's at a crisis home for women between the ages of sixteen and thirty-five. Sometimes it's herself she sees coming through the door.

Beth talks very openly about the past, but there is one person she has still never spoken to about what happened in 1967. Her daughter is in touch with her birth father, but not Beth. She hasn't talked to him since they were teenagers. "That's funny," she says, "because he just lives twenty doors up the street."

As for me, I had what I thought was an instant recovery. I was determined that this experience – all of it, the romance, the pregnancy, the child – would not affect me. I went back to Toronto for the rest of the summer. While I was there, I went to see the psychiatrist my mother had consulted. I found I had to make up things to say. I just wanted to get back to school, and I decided to return to Vancouver. There was one image I couldn't get out of my mind. It was from a Sunday afternoon when the Bursill-Halls had taken me on the spectacular highway drive from Vancouver to Squamish. It was as if I had, until then, completely missed the mountains and the sea; I had been so absorbed in myself that I had not seen the magnificence of the place where I was living. I wanted to go back and experience it. I also felt if I left Vancouver for good I would be giving in; that not going back would be an admission of failure.

So I did return, though I still knew very few people. I continued to be close to Hilary and Geoffrey. My letter-writing friend came back to UBC, too, but he seemed much less interested in me now that I wasn't in need of help. I continued at school, getting a graduate degree, and then I started to work in broadcasting. I think some of my ambition came from the determination to put it all behind me. But despite any success I had, I was always fearful and nervous. I often had what I called "emotional problems" – panic attacks and long bouts of anxiety. I wrote them down to overwork and general stress.

Like Linda and her mother, my family and I never discussed what had happened. It was a subject that silenced us all, even when it came very close to home. My mother became an actor later in her life, and a very successful one. Her first major stage and later film role was in a play called *Wedding in White*. One of the first successful, purely Canadian feature films, it told the story of a young working-class girl who gets pregnant during the Second World War in Toronto. Her parents marry her off to a friend of the family, an old man, to keep up appearances. My mother played the part of the mother to great acclaim, winning the Best Supporting Actress award in the first year of the Canadian Film Awards. But although we discussed the film many times, we never related it to ourselves as mother and daughter faced with much the same family crisis. Just before I got the idea for this book, as I was making a collage of her many press clippings to give her as a birthday gift, I found a still photograph from *Wedding in White* – my mother is stretching out her hand, almost touching the stomach of the girl who played her daughter. The emotion playing across the face of the actor is heartbreaking, yet it was nothing I had seen myself.

While writing all these pages and thinking so much about that time in my life, I have looked at that picture many times again, and I've started to see it differently. It is much more to me now than the souvenir of an award-winning performance. I do not believe that my mother's expression in the photograph is just acting, but that it is the pain she felt for me. It was a role that she did not have to take, one she could easily have refused because it was too close to her life. But she did choose it, and for this very private woman it was – though no one except she and my father could know – a public defence of her own daughter and the many other young women who had been shuffled off or hidden away. It was an act of love that I could not appreciate then. Her courage now takes my breath away.

But this is a recent revelation. For a very long time, I thought we had all agreed to forget, and I held to myself the secret and shame of the past. It was only when I passed the forty-year mark that I began to confront memories and emotions that I had deliberately stayed away from for years. At forty-two, I had just moved to a new city. I was there because of work, but I was not sure I had much else.

I began to assess my life and I didn't think it added up to a great deal. To others, I am sure it appeared to have glamour – a media career, a good salary, some public recognition. To me, they were not impressive achievements. When I added it up, a job, a house, and a dog were about all I had on the plus side. On the minus, I felt overwhelmed by a series of unsuccessful relationships that had led to no partner and no children. For more than twenty years I had run from any commitment, and when anyone asked about children, I would automatically say, "I'm too young." It was meant to get a laugh, but it was true. Even when I was forty, I didn't feel I had the emotional maturity to be a mother.

In an attempt to make a new life, I began to think about adoption and pursued it quite seriously for a while. But when I stopped to ask myself what I was really doing I was brought up short. I realized with a thud that I already had a child. I do not mean that I had forgotten. But I realized that I had not factored that past experience, however brief, of motherhood – the denial, the hiding, and the lost child – into the equation of my own loneliness and present despair.

At the same time, I knew it would be a mistake to launch a search for this child immediately. The first person I had to find was myself. Not only could I not approach this now grown-up person with a huge hole in my life for him to fill, I had to be ready to accept whatever I discovered. What if I couldn't find him? He might be dead. I might find someone I didn't like or who didn't like me. I had to be prepared for any outcome.

It took me a lot of questioning before I began to understand what had paralysed the emotional side of my life. When I was ready, several years later, to look for my child, I found the process quick and easy, as British Columbia had opened a registry service. Within a few weeks I had the name and telephone number of the child I had named Jonathan Clare.

The young man I met in the spring of 1993 was as nervous as I was, but we knew each other immediately. We have the same colouring, the same build. I like to think we have a shared sense of humour. He is also mature, well adjusted, and very happy; those are the gifts of the family that adopted him. They are exceptional people and they gave and continue to give him a wonderful life.

Two years later I went to his wedding, generously invited by his parents as a special guest to sit at their table. It was a lovely but difficult day, particularly at the end. On a movie screen that had been put up in the tennis court where everyone was dancing, slides of the bride and groom as children were continuously projected. Standing on the other side of the fence, looking through the wire mesh, I saw how separate our lives had been and what I had missed.

I do not know what the phrase "maternal feelings" means, but I do know that at our very first meeting, I understood for the first time the meaning of unconditional love. That has not changed, it has only grown richer. But I still do not know what to call myself or him in this relationship. Neither does he. Birth son and birth mother are the accepted terms, but they seem so clinical. There does not yet seem to be the right vocabulary. But if I have no words, I do have many more feelings. Recognizing and admitting the importance of what happened thirty years ago has given me back a part of myself that had simply atrophied during those months alone in the home. I have back the ability to feel both grief and joy – strong emotions that I had buried for many years.

—

Me, Beth, Linda, Marie, Loretta and Sherry, Judy and Karin – we are only a few of the thousands of women who have similar tales to tell. The details and the consequences of our stories are different for each of us, but I have not met one woman yet who came through being put away in a home for unwed mothers unaffected. Many have incorporated the experience into the work they do now. My search for subjects was completely random, but again and again I found women who now work with young, troubled girls. Many have gone into social work, and I have met several lawyers who chose family law, and a doctor who specialized in gynecology and obstetrics specifically because of the poor quality of treatment that she received as an unwed mother in a Calgary hospital in the mid-1960s.

Many, like this doctor, carry a great deal of anger with them. They cannot forgive the parents who "put them away," or the professionals who they believe forced them into giving up their children. They rage at the social mores that deemed them pariahs. And whether they found the home they stayed in a prison or refuge, they all hate the secrecy and hiding that served only to exaggerate their shame.

Perhaps it is because of my journalistic training, but I do not have that kind of anger. Rather, I am amazed at how quickly and dramatically the mores changed – of how distant a not very long ago past now seems. It is as if the shadow of shame disappeared in the first ray of sunlight. All of the women in this book were hidden away, quickly and thoroughly. For the girls who came after us, it was very different. The need to hide disappeared. The secret homes opened their doors.

# 9

## *Changing Times*

*"In the 1950's and 1960's there were waiting lists and a number
of building programs to increase bed capacities. One regional
director observed that the number now being served [in 1970]
is back to that of the early 50's in the homes."*
– "Analysis of Decreased Utilization of Salvation Army Maternity
Homes and Hospitals, 1976," Thesis, Lt.-Col Mary E. Verner

When I returned to Vancouver in the fall of 1967, I was immediately aware that the world had changed dramatically. New
ideas had been circulating in the air before then, but shut up in
my various hide-outs, I had no idea of how hard the wind had
blown. As I walked down Granville Street, I was surprised to
see that people my age even looked different – the girls with
long skirts and long hair, the boys with long hair and beads. It
had been the summer of love in Vancouver, and now all the
new ideas were coalescing into a new culture. I picked up a
copy of a tabloid paper that a skinny, bearded young man was
hawking on the street. In the *Georgia Straight* I read about
drugs, rock and roll, and of course sex. Sex was free love now
– sex wherever, whenever, and with whomever you wanted.

The taboo for a young, unmarried woman seemed to be to keep her virginity, not to lose it.

Just as my past had seemed unreal in the home, the home seemed unreal in the present, and it was as if my months there belonged to some ancient age. It was more than a strong wind, it was a hurricane of social change that was sweeping across society, almost obliterating the moral landscape in which I had so recently lived, demolishing the standards by which I and so many others had been so harshly judged.

Untangling the various forces that had been let loose is a wizard's job. Which came first? The pill? *Playboy* magazine? The ground-breaking work of Masters and Johnson? The insistence of a new young justice minister in Canada that the state had no business in the bedrooms of the nation? Whoever or whatever set off the explosions, everything was changing, including how we would deal with unmarried, pregnant girls and young women.

A few alarm bells had sounded early. The final recommendations that came out of the 1964 Out of Wedlock conference suggested that the homes might soon have to mount a rearguard action to protect their territory. There was, according to the final report, "a general feeling that these Homes for Unmarried Mothers should not be so cut off from the community and so isolated that no one knows about them." The conference, which had been organized by the United and Anglican churches, said that congregations should be "better informed about the Churches' overall concern for these girls, and how this is expressed in the availability of Homes." And in its suggestions for study and research, the final report sounded notes that would be heard everywhere by the end of the decade; subjects such as abortion and contraception should be studied, and so should changing attitudes to adoption. Consideration, the report said, should be given to "the need for providing supportive services to the unwed mother who keeps her baby. Among these are adequate financial assistance [and] day nurseries." Finally, perhaps in recognition of an emerging humanist morality where sex was concerned, the report noted, "In the overall service to a community, the need of a non-sectarian institution should be given consideration."

There is no record of whether or when these recommendations were implemented, but they were certainly prescient. The years 1969–70 were the watershed. As the 1970s rolled on, not only the age of the residents in the homes, but also their numbers decreased dramatically. By the end of the decade, the few homes that remained only remotely resembled the places that had hidden me and the other girls whose stories make up this book.

One doesn't need an historian to recount the obvious factors. The birth-control pill dramatically changed the demographic of unmarried pregnancies. Older girls, particularly middle-class and better-educated girls, were not the ones in trouble any more. The pill had been introduced in the early 1960s, but it was prescribed only to married women. That began to change even before the sale of contraception became legal in Canada in 1969, although, as historian Doug Owram reports in his book about the baby-boom generation, "gaining access to the Pill in the face of parents and conservative medical practitioners was, in some communities, more difficult than buying LSD or grass."

University campuses were among the first places to meet the demands of young women for the pill. In the winter of 1967, as I was entering Maywood, the student council at the University of Toronto took the daring step of distributing birth-control information. An investigative report by the Dalhousie University student newspaper in Halifax gives some indication of how girls found access to the new contraceptive. Apparently, the pill was very effective in treating acne. When the paper sent co-eds with perfect skin to the campus medical centre to ask for estrogen prescriptions, not one of them was turned down. As the American Salvation Army had to admit in a 1974 study, "contraception is listed as a contributing cause by all experts looking for causes for reduced occupancy in maternity homes."

In the same year that birth control was legalized, the Criminal Code of Canada was amended to allow for therapeutic abortions. Although it took some fudging with sympathetic doctors and hospital boards, there was now a safe and, at least in most big cities, an accessible recourse for women who did not wish to continue their pregnancies. The 1977 Badgely report on the application of the new abortion law noted that the trend of increasing "illegitimate live births" so clearly visible in the 1960s had dropped significantly since 1970. The authors gave abortion as one explanation.

There are contradictory figures from the United States that show births to unmarried girls actually increasing in the 1970s. But whether there were more or fewer unmarried mothers, they were not hidden away in homes. There was another enormous social change in the offing that was making the homes obsolete. The same conference that recommended consideration be given to providing supportive services, including financial assistance, to "the unwed mother who keeps her baby" was not expressing so much a new view of adoption, or an acknowledgement of the rights of unmarried mothers, but rather the looming problem of too many babies. Put crudely, the adoption market was glutted. There were more children available than there were people wanting to adopt. Dr. Mary Taylor, an American professor of social work at Ann Arbor, explained that there were relatively few couples in the prime twenty-five to forty age group because of the low birth rates in the 1930s. She urged her Canadian colleagues to face the facts: "For a generation social workers have been strongly encouraging girls who were pregnant out of wedlock to place their children for adoption. And we have done this with the very best of intentions [but] we are faced at this moment with the need to re-evaluate this advice because of the realities that face us. . . . Until we find some other alternatives, we'd better not separate children from their mothers, with no assurance that we will have any other mother to give them."

The old tune about the "best interests of the child" soon had new lyrics. The problems of placing children – which by the 1970s also included new regulations requiring more rigorous screening of potential adoptive parents – was no doubt a contributing factor, but the professionals also had to keep up with changing social attitudes. Well-publicized studies had by now shown that early marriages in order to "legitimate offspring . . . greatly increase the probability of marriage breakdown and its dissolution." At the same time, premarital sex was becoming more and more acceptable – an American Gallup poll showed that tolerance rates had increased 20 per cent from 1969 to 1974. The question begged: If a girl could have sex without shame, why could she not keep her baby without public disapproval? The social-work theorists now saw the issue differently than they had just a few years before. The young woman who had previously been deemed unfit to take on the responsibilities of a child was now encouraged to keep her baby and was even given state support to help her manage. The quick response of some governments may well have been defensive – Quebec instituted social aid to mothers the same year as therapeutic abortion became legal – but, nevertheless, it soon became possible in every province of Canada for an unmarried girl or woman to have access to financial resources that would allow her to keep and raise her child. A review of Ontario maternity homes in 1976 reported that 45 to 75 per cent of residents were deciding to keep their babies compared with 10 to 25 per cent a decade earlier. By 1982, 84 per cent of unmarried girls in Canada were leaving hospitals with their babies, a complete

The girls were getting younger and more restless. They wouldn't put up with the kind of strict rules that had been enforced previously. The report noted, "Of particular interest during the past year is the fact that while the girls coming to us for help are getting younger all the time, there is a decreasing need for rules and regulations to govern their behaviour. One would expect the reverse to be true. During the year, however, it has been necessary for us to work continually at liberalizing the restrictions on such matters as how often the girls may date, what should be considered proper attire in the house, and so on. Were it not for our ability to form and implement change speedily within the house itself, this past year would have seen us sadly outdated and providing a refuge scarcely resembling life in the outside world."

Some of the homes adapted radically to what they saw as the new needs of the unmarried mother. Instead of hiding girls, they now acted to support them in the move to single motherhood. Dormitories that had housed dozens of girls were changed into private rooms where a girl and her baby could spend their first months together as she prepared to cope with her new responsibilities. The Salvation Army took a leadership role with the changes it made to places such as the Bethany Home in downtown Toronto. A historian of that home noted in 1994 the changes that began in the 1970s: "No longer is the client solely looking for a confidential environment to reside at while she awaits the birth of her child. She is now in need of so many other services – counseling, education and general lifeskills. Many of the women who now come to Bethany Homes, about 95%, have been abused either physically, emotionally or sexually, and thus are in need of a warm, caring environment to help her begin to deal with the feelings and fears that these life experiences have left her with." By the mid-1970s the Maywood Home in Vancouver saw the same kind of transformation. A mother-baby program was started and a family worker was hired to assist the girls with baby and other homemaking skills. In one of those ironic twists of time, girls were once again coming back from the hospital to the home with their babies. But now it was not a required stay, nor would a girl wake up one morning, as Janet Roberts did, to find her child had been taken away.

The Roman Catholic Church fashioned a new role for itself out of a slightly different necessity. The fear of losing babies through abortion gave those who supported the Church's homes renewed purpose. At the same time, their work became much harder financially. Because they did not support the United Way's funding of planned parenthood organizations, the Catholic homes, such as Rosalie Hall in Scarborough, often withdrew from the organization, making themselves completely self-supporting. Internally they also had to make dramatic changes. Young girls would not come to a home to be judged any more. Now they expected an atmosphere of love and acceptance and assistance with making plans for a future that included their child. Rosalie Hall is still a going concern. Villa Rosa was opened in Winnipeg in the 1970s. The Misericordia order no longer has the half-dozen homes it did in the 1950s and 1960s, but it is still busy, providing young single mothers with day care and other resources they need to keep their children.

The remaining Catholic and Salvation Army residences are few compared to the number they had in the 1950s and 1960s. Most of those homes, as well as the dozens run by other denominations and religious organizations, could not, or did not choose, to survive. In part, this was because they were no longer welcomed by governments. Social-service policy makers wanted professionals, not volunteers, to run institutions that were being given tax dollars. Women such as Molly Breen had no training, and the churches were suspect. A 1979 report on the future of maternity homes in Ontario pointed out that as residents were getting younger they "require more skilled help than is available in most of the homes for unmarried mothers." Social workers had always been disturbed by the missionary zeal that was still at the heart of many homes. Now with the decreases in occupancy and with so many homes apparently foundering, they could make their point more strongly. Casework, not morality, should be the approach. Professional standards should be enforced, and trained staff should be paid professional salaries. The homes, the report went on to say, had been the "most 'efficiently' operated children's institutions in the province," because they had paid their staff low or no wages. Most of the Army officers and religious Sisters were paid only a nominal sum, and trained staff were hired for half the average starting salary in comparable children's service agencies. If the homes were to stay in business, they would have to pay market wages.

In the same report the criticisms of the homes continued. The "staff–resident ratios were weak," the buildings were the "wrong size and type," and no funding had been directed to "research and development." The homes had not been able to "adapt and change programme approaches in keeping with the new social values and social trends of the 1970s." There was hope, however, the report said, in that "maternity homes are in many ways a most logical and experienced group to encourage to deliver priority programmes related to 'prevention' and 'family crisis' supports. With a clear mandate and appropriate resources, most of them could develop an excellent, comprehensive package of reduced residential and maternity-related programmes beginning in the next few years."

The sponsors of the homes were not eager to pick up the bone they had been tossed. The cost of coming up to the new government standards was prohibitive, and there was also a simple lack of enthusiasm. As one retired brigadier from the Salvation Army put it, "I enjoyed it when I was there [in the 1950s and 1960s], but now I wonder if my life's work was any good, the way they're pulling it apart. What I mean by pulling it apart is that all the work we did seems to be to no avail, doesn't it? People have babies and abortions, and just take it for granted. They live together and think it's natural. But it isn't. It's spoiling the morale [sic]. I don't know what happened to the morale. It's sad. It'll come back again. Because back in the Bible days, when they did things like this, if you read the history, you'll know that terrible things happened and suddenly they came back to the proper way of life."

Of the twenty or more homes that had been operating in Ontario at the peak of the demand years, by the mid-1970s only nine remained as residential institutions and all but five of them, according to the 1979 report, had "diversified their program missions because of utilization pressures." In other words, a lack of clients had forced them to change. The report's recommendations to government listed further cuts to the remaining homes. The Salvation Army's Bethany Home in Ottawa, with a utilization rate of only 30 per cent, was told to cut half its beds; the same for Grace Haven in Hamilton. The Army's Bethesda Home in London, Ontario, should be closed completely. The United Church–affiliated Victor Home would lose a quarter of its capacity. The Anglicans reduced services at their St. Monica Home in Kitchener and, by the end of the decade, had closed Humewood House in downtown Toronto.

It was the same story right across the country, as homes either changed their focus to serve new social needs or simply closed. In British Columbia, the Burnaby Home for Girls operated by the United Church, after expanding in the mid-1960s, closed completely in 1973. In Edmonton, the evangelical Christian women who ran the Beulah Home closed it down in the late 1960s. Pineview, the new home that Sister Frances Cabrini had built to replace the old Misericordia, was taken over by the city in 1973 to use for other purposes. The Salvation Army homes across the prairies had changed their mandates by the mid-1970s in the same way that the Bethany Home had in Toronto. In Winnipeg, the Army closed its old residence for girls only and replaced it with Linden View, a shelter for people with a variety of needs, which the Army ran cooperatively with several other social-service agencies in the city.

Montreal had at least nine homes open between 1950 and 1969. The next decade saw all of them give up their secrecy and many of them close, including Villa St-Michel, where Marie Benoit had stayed. In the Atlantic provinces, the half-dozen or more homes in the region are all gone. Their passing was not particularly marked, as so few people knew that they had been there at all. Perhaps they had done their job too well.

---

Until I started this book, I had never gone back to the Maywood Home for Girls. It was hard to avoid completely as it lay on my route to the airport. At first I would deliberately look away, later I would glance quickly at it, wondering if I would see one of them/us/me going in or out of the gate. I never did see anyone, and until I watched that brief movie scene of a home for unwed mothers in the 1930s, I had not thought or cared about what had happened to the place or the people.

When I began to think about writing stories from these homes, I went back to Maywood. It was another grey Vancouver day, this time in November, and it felt no different than that wet March afternoon more than thirty years earlier. The building that I had for a moment thought might be a Victorian mansion was still there, and was still an unromantic two-storey block of 1950s modernism. I had learned from my preliminary research for the book that Maywood had changed its mission in the mid-1970s to train girls for motherhood rather than to hide them from a judging public, but that was all I knew. As I walked up to the front door I saw a hand-lettered sign: "The Maywood Home for Girls is closed. Please inquire next door."

Just behind me, where the Big House used to be – where the officers used to live – was a new structure. I knew as I walked over what it must be. This low, rounded building with large front windows was much more attractive than my old home had been. Of course it wouldn't be a new place for unwed mothers. Pregnant, single women do not have to hide any more. It would have to be a home for this era. And it was, as I had expected, a shelter for battered women.

So Maywood has come full circle. But now it is, or it seems to me, the true shelter and refuge that it was not thirty years ago. When I was there in 1967, it only protected the public from the sight of the bulging bellies of girls they did not want to have among them. Now the new home truly does protect women from very real danger and violence.

Sterling, the home in Oakville, Ontario, where Karin and Judy came in the fall of 1964, is now also a sanctuary for victims of domestic abuse. In 1976, the Ontario government reported that maternity referrals to Sterling were negligible, and it, too, adapted quickly to new needs. It first became a home for troubled and delinquent adolescents, then in the early 1990s addressed the new needs of women. Today, its location is even more secret than it was when unmarried girls flocked there in the 1950s and 1960s, but like Maywood, now it is secret for a good reason. I have quite happily changed the name of this home in the book to protect the safety of the women who are there now.

I had heard so much about the beauty of Sterling that I wanted to see it for myself, and on one lush summer afternoon Karin and I drove out the thirty or so miles from Toronto, taking the same route that she had with her parents so long ago. Today a major highway takes you there, not the two-lane road that the Sorensens navigated. The main street of Oakville, where Karin and Judy waited for the bus one Saturday afternoon to take them to the big city for Christmas shopping, is now crammed with boutiques and chic restaurants.

As we drove in through the stone gateposts at the entrance-way to Sterling, I had to agree that all the descriptions were right. It is not so much a mansion as a large and graceful house, spread out gently over half an acre or so, spoiled only by the modern dormitory that was attached to house the influx of girls Sterling took in. The grounds are almost unchanged. There is still a sunken formal garden at the front, cornered with large flower-filled urns. The fishpond is still there, although the Chinese bridge has crumbled. As Karin had said so accurately, "It was a nice place to hide, if you had to hide."

We went up the front steps to the huge porch and the leaded-glass double doors. Our ring was answered by a security guard who told us that there had been other visits from other women trying to mend their fractured pasts. As we walked through the front part of the house, Karin's memory began to work. The "morgue" – the formal visiting room – was now cosy, with comfy chintz couches and kids' toys. The dining room, which had been elegant but severe with its dark-oak panelling, now had personal touches, too – a hutch of china dishes, plates propped on a high rail that ran around the room. What once was the chapel is now a TV room.

When she first got out of the car, Karin had said she felt nervous coming back. But once inside the house, it was her lack of feeling that struck her. Although the place held so many memories, she felt like an observer, a historian pointing out this and that, but without any attachment to what she was seeing. She even tried a few jokes about the number of potatoes she must have peeled in the old-fashioned kitchen, but they fell flat. It was as if she had put the past away, locked and secure. At least for now she could not, or would not, open any emotional doors.

The Bethel Home where Janet Roberts stayed for almost seven months in 1957 is also still standing, but Kennedy Road, which Janet remembered as a country road, is now a major thorough-fare in Scarborough, and the old brick farmhouse looks very different. It had become too small by the early 1960s, and the Pentecostal Church raised money to build a new home in Agincourt that opened in 1964. Since then, the old Bethel Home has had new owners, who have added two large wings to either side of the original building. Along the front is a white peaked-roof porch held up by a dozen ante-bellum white columns. The Bethel is still a home – but now it's a modern funeral home.

Janet went back to see the Bethel Home in 1991 just before she took early retirement from the Scarborough Social Services Department. Although her last position had been in an office just up the street from the old home, for years she avoided that part of Kennedy Road. But when she knew she wouldn't be back, she decided she wanted to take a last look at the past. With a friend from work along for moral support, she retraced her steps from 1957. Standing in front of the old home, she pointed out to her friend her upstairs bedroom window, now almost hidden by the new porch. Inside, she saw the old wooden floors she used to polish, and she could still make out part of the original floor plan – the present coffee room was a part of the country kitchen, where she had done so much cooking and canning. The old, bad memories and anger at what she had lost here welled up. Janet didn't want to see any more.

I went there myself in the summer of 1997. The young and friendly funeral director who saw me wandering around out-side was glad to tell me what he knew about the history of the building. Originally it had been a mushroom farm, and the first owners had lived there until the building was sold to the Pentecostal Church. The bowling alley had been built for the family and the migrant workers who came in the spring and fall. The main floor of the old home was now completely redone. Only the third floor – where my guide had himself lived as a student apprentice – is as it was. Proud of his establishment, he took time to show me around. It is a light and airy building now, not like the sparse place that Janet had known with its front rooms where the girls weren't allowed. In the basement there is now a comfortable sitting room and a small playroom for young children. The toys and tiny table and chairs are a thoughtful touch in a place that could so easily be gloomy and forbidding. Though the present use of the house on Kennedy Road might seem morbid, it is a much more warm and welcoming place now than when it ministered, without much compassion, to the grief and loss of so many young girls and women.

Loretta Fournier did go back to the Misericordia, at least to the hospital. She had her other two children there. With a ring on her finger and a husband beside her, it was a different experience altogether. "They treated me like a queen then," she says. "It was the best of everything." But now the big stone hospital is only a memory. The Misericordia was torn down when the Sisters decided to rebuild in the early 1970s. The laundry building, where so many pregnant girls had been hidden on the second floor behind tiny, covered windows, became a pile of rubble. The site is now the Eric Cormack Centre, an institution for profoundly disabled children. As Sherry said, "It's sad to think all the misery that has gone on there." You can still walk to the riverbank just a block away. I asked Sherry if she would go back there for me and record what it was like to be there now. She wrote, "Things have changed since 1957. There are still the purple-headed thistles that I remember having to avoid where we would rest on the guardrail posts overlooking the river. And there are so many more buildings now across the river. Where the market garden used to be on the flats below, there's now an arena. And where there was just the old path, now there is a mini-park and a bench to sit on. As I sit here writing, behind me are roses, petunias and marigolds. It's summer. No suicide plans to make today."

By 1963, Sister Frances had got her new home, complete with new name – Pineview. The building was owned by the provincial government and leased back to the order for a dollar a year. But "differences" arose between the Sisters and the government in the late 1960s. Until that time the Sisters had interviewed girls looking for a place to stay and had made their own decisions about who would be suitable for Pineview. Now the provincial Department of Welfare wanted its social workers to determine where a girl should be placed. Even more insulting to the order, the government wanted the Sisters to switch from working with unmarried mothers to caring for children and serving juvenile delinquents. Instead, the Misericordia Sisters left Alberta, and Pineview was closed. *The Western Catholic Reporter*, in a story headlined "Sister Frances Cabrini Leaves: Alberta Poorer," noted that "before she left on December 21 Sister Frances was honored by the City of Edmonton at a private luncheon with Mayor Ivor Dent as host."

In Montreal, Les Soeurs de la Miséricorde also saw their four homes change or close one by one. The original downtown residence had so many bad associations that at the end of the 1960s, they moved to a new location and gave the place a new name, Service Sociale Ville-Marie. Villa St-Michel, the second home that Marie Benoit went to, remained open, but by the middle of the 1970s, there weren't enough girls to fill the huge building that had once had a hundred or more beds. It became and remains a community centre.

The old Miséricorde is still standing, stony and severe on St-Hubert, just south of René Lévesque Boulevard. When Marie moved back to Montreal in 1995 after being away for many years, she asked her husband to drive her by the home. She had planned to get out of the car and look around, but she stayed glued to the front seat. A year later she went back again with her daughter, who wanted to see where her mother had stayed until she was frightened away by the story of the employer who assaulted one of the Miséricorde girls. Even then, Marie could only walk around the outside of the old complex, pointing out the back building with its tiers of iron balconies where she used to sometimes see the little children standing behind the railings as they waited to be adopted. But she couldn't go up those front stairs and in the door as she had thirty years ago. That was too much.

I did climb those stairs. From the sign outside I knew that this building was now the St-Vigier Centre, a long-term-care centre for the elderly and disabled. Inside, the front lobby has clearly been remodelled – the high ceiling has been lowered and there is no sign of the nuns' office that Marie was first taken to. But just off the lobby, I found the tiny elevator that she had taken up to the dormitory floor. Down the hall, the large, ornate chapel with its tiers of balconies seemed unchanged. But there were no pregnant girls anywhere. Now the corridors are filled with wheelchairs and twisted bodies. There is no more joy there than there ever was.

Linda Chalmers had deliberately stayed away from Stanley Street and the home whose name she could never remember. She was close to it often enough, shopping down on Sherbrooke Street, but she always hurried past the street that went up the hill to the old brownstone. Whenever I talked to Linda for this book, she was frustrated that she couldn't bring the name of the place to mind. But as we gradually rooted around the past – this was the first time Linda had told her story to anyone – she decided to go back.

She went with her new husband for support. She recognized the house on the east side of the street right away. The three Greek letters hanging under the big, bowed front window told her what it was now, and the friendly young man who answered the door confirmed it was a fraternity house. He thought maybe it used to be "a home for rich girls that got pregnant." Linda didn't want to go in, but over his shoulder she could see into the old front room. "There was a big pool table there now. I had to laugh, thinking about how it used to be when I was there. And now here were all these horny young guys hitting balls around. It is funny." Later, I tried to research the address. The house had been owned by the Catholic Welfare Bureau, but the agency had been reorganized in the mid-1960s and nobody knew anything about the place on Stanley Street.

Molly Breen's old house is still standing in St. John's. By coincidence it was just down the street from the bed and breakfast on Gower Street I stayed at when I went to Newfoundland to meet Beth. Although this area – just up from the harbour and near the Hotel Newfoundland – is gradually becoming upscale, Molly's place hasn't received any gentrifying touches. Aside from a utilitarian coat of dark-red paint, its plain, wooden three-storey front is unchanged. The block it stands in on Wood Street is still mostly rooming houses. Beth and I had to go back several times before somebody finally answered the door of number 18. We had heard that the occupants were mostly mentally ill men who had been released from institutions, and the confusion of the young man who answered the door seemed to confirm this. Leading off from the hall was the narrow staircase where Herb

Breen used to sit as the girls stepped around him on their way up and down, but everything else was blocked off and chopped up into rental rooms. Beth went up the stairs anyway, trying to sniff out something from so many years ago. "That's where my room was," she said, and knocked on a door. It took about five minutes, but eventually a middle-aged, unshaven man came to the door in his underwear. He couldn't make out what we were talking about. It was time to leave the past behind.

Molly had owned the house, but after Herb died in 1969 she didn't really want to be there any more. And as was the case everywhere else, there were fewer and fewer girls who needed a place to stay and hide. Molly packed up and sold. She lived in New York for a while with a sister, but she missed St. John's. She came back to cook, this time for royalty. She was in the kitchen at Government House and takes great pride in telling how she once made dinner for the Queen.

At eighty-five, Molly is still going strong. She has bad arthritis in her knees, but she still manages to get around pretty well. When we visited, it was no surprise that the smell of baking came to the door with Molly. She had just put one of her specialties into the oven, a brown molasses cake.

—

Homes for unwed mothers, as I knew them – as the women in this book knew them in the 1950s and 1960s – are gone now. So, if girls do not need to hide any more, if they are no longer put away so their big bellies will not offend public morality, is there, aside from historical curiosity, any present point in remembering them? Do these places and the way we treated girls and young women then have any resonance for us now?

I think so. In many ways I do not think we have come very far. Or, rather, we went a distance and now have stopped, tempted to turn back. Not perhaps to the secrecy and punishment of the past, but I fear we may be perilously close to the social attitudes that lead there.

A young woman – or, for that matter, one in her thirties or forties – can now choose to raise her baby by herself. She may not be nominated for mother of the year, but neither is she a social pariah. With the support of good friends and family, she can make it on her own. She can rent an apartment, hold down a job, and find day care. She has a good chance of doing the best for her child.

The problem now – at least it is defined that way – is pregnant *teenagers*, "the babies having babies," as the magazine covers tell us over and over again. The latest Statistics Canada numbers published in late 1997 lead to media reports about an "alarming" rise in the number of young pregnant girls. In fact, even though the rates have increased in the last half-dozen years – after a significant drop during the 1970s and 1980s – they are still substantially lower than in the 1950s and 1960s. There is a good deal of "perception" at work now. In the open world of the 1990s, the old "unwed mother" is simply more visible; we do not have the sham of shotgun weddings and we do not hide her away from public view in secluded and secretive homes any more.

But if there has been a recent rise, let us indeed take that seriously. It certainly does seem to be true that young people are sexually active at much younger ages. Although birth control is – we are led to believe – easy to obtain, many teenagers abstain from protection. The abortion rate is substantial (though without numbers for the secret, illegal abortions of the past it is hard to know what that increase really is), but abortion seems to be the choice of mostly older teens and young women. Many young, sometimes very young, girls are carrying their babies to term and, for the most part, are keeping them.

It is definitely progress that we no longer hide or punish these girls – or, without concern for their wishes and feelings, take their children from them. But, nevertheless, these very young new mothers, often completely on their own, present real concerns we must address. Those who monitor tax dollars say it is simply too expensive to give them financial assistance and expensive social services. But money is a red herring. Even with the most generous subsidies and support systems, the question remains whether such a young girl can give herself and her child the stability they both need. Perhaps a few can, but many pregnant teenagers come out of violent and abusive families and patterns of behaviour they are at risk of repeating on their own. The big question that liberals and conservatives alike must address is whether we – and they – are really looking for the best for mother and baby. Because it is us – society – as much as the girls themselves, who are encouraging these girls to become young single parents. The pendulum seems to have made its classic swing completely to the other side, so that now girls seem to be under great pressure again – but now the pressure is for them to keep their children. I found that this concern came up in many of my conversations with the women whose stories fill this book. Although they envy the freedom unmarried girls have now to keep their children, many wondered whether these girls can possibly be ready to be mothers. Those whose own children were adopted do not like the way it was done, but many of them still feel that they were not ready for motherhood.

The solutions offered today raise their own problems. Abortion is safe and legal, but it is not the quick and convenient panacea that it was once believed to be. Now that it is an option, abortion has become a complex moral issue, and the decision whether to abort is often clouded and made more difficult by the spokespeople on both sides of the debate.

As far as adoption goes, even though new reproductive technology has given many more people the opportunity to have their own biological children, there is still a demand for babies by couples anxious to have a family. But few girls seem to choose to give up their child to new parents. Besides the social pressure "to keep," even if a girl is thinking of adoption, she – and everyone else involved – faces unknown consequences, which do not make adoption an answer to the problem of teenage single motherhood.

It is clear that we cannot go back to the closed and secret adoptions of the past as an alternative to girls keeping their children. The many reunions we see today and the desperate desire of so many birth mothers and adoptees to find each other make that option an illusion.

Open adoption has become the buzz word of activists. It is an attractive theory, but it has yet to be proven over any length of time. Can all parties really be expected to act in the best interests of each other all the time, or will self-interest inevitably interfere? I wonder how I might have acted in times of loneliness or confusion if I had had easy access to the child I had given to the care of others. To be fair to all, open adoptions would have to be closely monitored by social-service intermediaries or counsellors. This raises the question of cost and also privacy. Do we really want to keep a watch on people in this way?

I think there are lessons from the past that we can apply today, if only cautionary ones. It is important to look back because the way the problem of teenage pregnancy is being framed today has many familiar echoes.

It seems we are very close to blaming the girls again. In his "Contract with America," then Speaker of the House Newt Gingrich lumped teenage mothers in with criminals and immigrants as examples of those whose soft treatment under "liberals" was part of the fall of his country's greatness. The Heritage

Foundation in the States declares unequivocally, as part of its mandate, that "the primary goal of conservative reform [is]: To wipe out the scourge of illegitimacy in the United States." In a 1996 issue of *Commentary* magazine, American social psychologist Charles Murrary wrote, "Illegitimacy is the single most important social problem of our time – more important than crime, drugs, poverty, illiteracy, or homelessness because it drives everything else."

According to this analysis, the delinquent should be punished. And so in the States, again thanks to Gingrich and his "Personal Responsibility Act," we see unmarried mothers being denied or cut off welfare.

The same approaches, at least in some public and political discussions, are gaining in popularity in our own country. Once again, it is the girl's fault and she must pay. The second part of the baby equation – the old "putative father" – seems as elusive and unimportant as ever.

We may be headed once more in the direction of hiding. I cannot believe we will hide the girls again, but are we not – by suggesting that we are being too soft – hiding the problem? Or hiding from the problem?

Simply to make it more difficult for girls to look after their babies and to constantly remind them and everyone else that they are not capable of being mothers will only cause, I believe, what the moralist of the past caused: shame and anger.

Shame may have its place, but surely not here. Will girls and boys stop having sex? They haven't yet. We cannot legislate hormones. That does not mean there cannot be change, however. As tired as it may sound, we do have to look at the causes. We might begin with the disastrous families that many of these children come from. How often is a pregnancy the only option for a girl to escape an unbearable situation? Or at least one way to prove to herself that she can do at least one thing right?

Why don't young people use birth control? Is it less available than we think? Is it promoted only in such a clinical way that it evades or avoids the complex personal decisions that a girl and her partner need to make before they cross that traumatic border between childhood and adult responsibility? Do we really talk about sex any more openly than we used to? In interviews that I did with them for the CBC Newsworld series "Century," Virginia Johnson and Dr. William Masters, those pioneers of sexual health, said that they see us backsliding to a fearful and secretive attitude to sexuality. Parents want to control what their children learn about sex, but are they taking on the responsibility of real communication with their kids? There does not seem to be a great deal of evidence that they are.

I am not suggesting that we simply accept teenage sexual activity and find ways to make it less of a social problem. Abstinence is a valid choice, one that makes a great deal of sense for many young people. But it should not have to lead to a repressive, anxious journey through adolescence. As the feminist Naomi Wolfe suggested in her recent study of teenage sexuality, *Promiscuities*, perhaps we should consider teaching children gradual sexuality, making them aware of the options besides intercourse that are available to them. It doesn't matter who teaches them, parents or schools, but we must deal with the subject in a manner that acknowledges the reality of teenage life today.

Those who provided a solution in the decades when I was a young person may have thought they had the best intentions. But they also caused great harm, from the brutality of charging a fourteen-year-old rape victim with promiscuity to the slight but real humiliation of making a twenty-year-old woman clean bathrooms. In spite of the personal warmth and kindness on the part of many staff in the homes, the girls were still stripped of their dignity, self-respect, and – literally – identity. The harm done was the result of a code of judgement and punishment based not on understanding but on righteousness. While the secretive homes for unwed mothers no longer exist, much of the attitude that brought them into being seems to be coming back. We are in danger of allowing insensitivity, sexual insecurity, disinformation, and moral superiority to propel us – individuals and institutions alike – into positions of harshness and absurdity. The stories that I have told should remind us how low we can sink in the name of virtue, morality, and family values, of how heartless we can be when even our kindness is based on rigid and exclusive moralizing.

If in hearing these stories, we feel some embarrassment at how we once treated these young women, perhaps we will think twice about how we deal with them now.

# ACKNOWLEDGEMENTS

Unfortunately, because I have had to change their names, I cannot thank publicly the people who were most important to the making of this book – the women whose stories fill these pages. But my gratitude to them is immense, for the time they gave me and the honesty they shared. They began as strangers to me. I count all of them now as friends.

Many of them became unofficial researchers for this book, guiding me to other women and digging up information on the homes they had stayed in. "Karin," in particular, turned into a real pro. Because so much of this information was scattered across the country, hidden or long forgotten in libraries and archives, I also had to rely on official researchers. Penny Lee Colborne and Donna Korchinski continually surprised me with what they found. If they ever leave journalism, they should open up detective agencies. Kimberley Ducey started out transcribing tapes for me and ended up being a hound dog, finding sources that I could not even imagine. Martha Muzychka was my special guide to Newfoundland. Willa Marcus gave me many useful leads, particularly to Andrea Nemeth and the unpublished graduate work she had done on the early days of maternity homes in Toronto. I would also like especially to thank former staff members from a number of homes who generously shared their memories with me.

From the very germination of this book, I had the luck to have Beverley Slopen as my literary agent. The enthusiasm of Avie Bennett and Doug Gibson made McClelland & Stewart the only publishers to go with. My editor, Dinah Forbes, managed to read my first drafts without gagging and pushed me exactly when and where I needed it. With a day job like mine, it's difficult to find time for writing, but Fred Youngs of CBC Newsworld immediately understood and found me the weeks I needed to get this project finished. Nijole Kuzmickas read the manuscript and gave me much good advice. So did Karin Klassen (not the "Karin" in this book). My partner, Maurice Yacowar, was always there to keep me laughing (e.g., *Ammo vincit omnia*).

But most of all I would like to thank my parents, Doris and Harry Petrie. I know it has been difficult for them to have our private lives the possible subject of public discussion. But – as always – they have fully supported me in what I thought was right to do.